# SCENES FROM THE END

On a parapet of Hitler's abandoned Eagle's Nest, May 1945

# SCENES
### THE LAST DAYS
# FROM
### OF WORLD WAR II
# THE END
### IN EUROPE

# FRANK E. MANUEL

STEERFORTH PRESS
SOUTH ROYALTON, VERMONT

For information about permission to reproduce
selections from this book, write to:
STEERFORTH PRESS L.C., P.O. Box 70,
South Royalton, Vermont 05068


Library of Congress Cataloging-in-Publication Data

Manuel, Frank Edward
Scenes from the end : the last days of World War II in Europe / Frank E. Manuel.
p. cm.
ISBN 1–883642–55–8 (alk. paper)
1. World War, 1939–1945—Europe. I. Title.

D755.7.M36 2000
940.53 21—dc21    99–043516
CIP


FIRST EDITION

# CONTENTS

# PROEM

**A** THIRTY-FOUR-YEAR-OLD American intelligence officer, I became a prisoner-of-war interrogator with the Twenty-first Corps of the United States Army and witness to the endgame of the Third Reich. Our troop movements were often so rapid that tactical information elicited from the German soldiers, who were surrendering to us in droves, quickly became obsolete, and my role at headquarters turned into that of a supernumerary assigned to a variety of tasks for which I had no previous training. On Hitler's birthday, April 20, 1945, I was promoted to first lieutenant and awarded a Bronze Star for meritorious service against the enemy. Toward the end, medals were distributed among us officers in profusion.

Notes written immediately after I returned home, on V-J night, were composed in a frenzied attempt to recapture what I had seen and heard during the last stages of the war in Europe. Fifty years later I found these papers, along with letters to my wife, then working in Washington. Excerpts from the letters are a documentary record of what I felt and thought at the time, censored by a writer who was subject to the constraints of military security and conjugal vows. Conversations reported here have passed through the smoke screen of memory, recollections of the spirit, rather than the precise detail, of events; sometimes they echo the voices of other observers. Converse with the defeated enemies in the last months of the war on the western front was rarely subject to the formalities of interrogation; the quotations and descriptions are the distilled essence of those encounters. Prisoners of war often had a greater need to talk than we had a capacity to listen. In the long, drawn-out dialogues between us more truths were conveyed than in the casual exchanges of most men during times of peace. The style and technique of these sketches derive from the movies, with their abrupt shifts of scenes and persons, to which the reader has to adapt. Military historians have assembled a picture of the grand design, creating the myth of an official history; but fragments may be closer to the chaos of experience in war before it has been subjected to cleansing.

Fact and an occasional fantasy rub shoulders in my story of the collapse of the Reich, seen through a tiny peephole. The names of minor characters are synthetic, but the major players are depicted as I confronted them. To blur the line between invention and recollection, fantasy and memory, was not my intent; it just happened that way. The result is a hybrid far more common among historians since Herodotus than we professionals admit when we don our academic gowns. What I have written is sometimes a "feigned history" in the spirit of David Hume rather than Leopold von Ranke's pretentious manifesto, *bloss wie es eigentlich gewesen war* (simply as it actually happened).

*Mea culpa.* Today I feel ashamed of verdicts pronounced in the heat of battle or at the sight of human atrocities. I regret the summary judgments that poured out of me and the sentiments of superior virtue that besmirch all victors.

# INTRODUCTION

EW OF THE LOCAL AMENITIES existed or were accessible to my parents when they settled in Boston's West End in the first decade of the century (though a streetcar line was built in 1910, the year of my birth), and they soon abandoned its noisy, crowded streets, to join the trek of Jewish immigrants to the green pastures of Dorchester and Roxbury. The Jews prospered in their new, more placid neighborhoods, profiting from the expanding economy of the World War I years, and there their children reached adulthood. We graduated from elementary schools run by shrewd Irish spinsters who maintained discipline through discreet application of a rattan switch in the privacy of a cloakroom. The more proficient students went on to Boston Latin School, and in due course on to Harvard.

The curriculum in Boston Latin was based on the study of languages and literature, to the neglect of science. And when I landed at Harvard I continued my literary studies, along with polishing the oratorical skills I had exhibited at a very early age. In sermons delivered in Yiddish or Hebrew in a Roxbury synagogue on Sabbath afternoons I displayed my prowess — and won the resentment of my peers.

The pogroms in Eastern Europe that followed World War I had heightened Jewish consciousness, and the rise of fascism in its German form in the 1930s brought into the fold assimilated Jews who were members of Reform synagogues in the wealthier suburbs of Boston such as Brookline and Newton. A Board of Jewish Education expanded the traditional charitable Jewish functions, which had concentrated on the aged and the impoverished, and founded a Hebrew College, giving young Jews an opportunity to continue Hebraic studies on a level as sophisticated as that of Harvard courses. My days were divided between two establishments of higher learning that vied with each other for my time and interest. Complicating further my intellectual adolescence was the Jewish trade union movement, in which my father played a significant role. My soul was thus fragmented by allegiance to trade unionism tainted with radical politics; enthusiasm for Zionism, its propaganda enhanced by the Balfour Declaration; occasional ritual observance of traditional Judaism; and absorption with new fields of thought opened up by my college studies.

Harvard generously awarded me traveling fellowships that exposed me to the performances of an enraged, screaming Hitler and the nascent fascism that seemed bewitched by his oratory. Back in Boston after a European sojourn, I found an academic market shriveled by the Great Depression. After some patchwork appointments leading nowhere, I saw an outlet for my explosive energies in journalism, and undertook to be a correspondent in Spain for *The Nation*. My prediction of an imminent clash between the defenders of the republic and the phalangists went unheeded, and when the civil war broke out I was on my way to France and the United States. As the war continued, I turned into an ardent protagonist for the Loyalist cause. During a debate in Boston's Copley Plaza Hotel I caught the attention of Felix Frankfurter, and he used his good offices in Washington to have me installed as regional director of the Federal Writers' Project. I thus joined the cohort of Roosevelt's New Dealers, an invasion of academics, including Jews, who were something of a novelty in the halls of government. World War II had broken out in Europe, and we were in the vanguard of civilians active in enlisting the United States on the side of the British and the defeated French. After leaving the Writers' Project I repaired to the capital, which was already humming with activity and where I discharged diverse functions related to preparing America for combat and ensuring victory: I barnstormed around the country, hoping to convert with my impassioned speeches groups who were not happy at the prospect of an American entry into the war; as that eventuality came closer and was then realized, I shifted my efforts to the Office of Price Administration, where we aimed to attract workers to critical industries by stabilizing their rents. In a few months we created a unique vocabulary of "defense rental areas," "in-migrants," "out-migrants," and "major capital improvements" to judge the merits of landlords' petitions for rent increases. Never had I worked so hard, and the zeal with which I defended our regulations was notorious. Twitted because my scholarly training had not included courses in real estate, about which I admitted total ignorance, I would retort saucily that one needn't be a lion to be a lion tamer.

Except for a brief stint at the Office of War Information, where I listened aimlessly to long handouts designed to counter Nazi propaganda, I remained among the administrators of price controls until 1943. But with our manpower and economy now wholly committed to the war, there were mutterings about draft dodgers and scores of us joined the armed forces. Before I had a chance to convince the navy of my fitness for a commission, the army snatched me away to Camp Barkeley in the heart of Texas, where I learned the rudiments of basic training as a private. My excess weight and bureaucratic sloth made it hard for me to keep pace with far younger men. I was moved about from Clerk's School, where my atrocious typing could have only retarded the war effort, to the Medical Corps, for which my Harvard doctorate in the history of ideas was no preparation. Finally I was sent to Camp Ritchie, the Military Intelligence Training Center in Maryland, where I was taught how to interrogate French-speaking prisoners. But our troops were advancing rapidly and it was decreed I be retrained as an interrogator of German prisoners. After the passage of months I was commissioned a second lieutenant and shipped out to England, where this memoir begins.

From "somewhere in England" in November 1944, as Roosevelt's re-election for his fourth and last term was being celebrated in the Allied world, I wrote the first in a series of letters to my wife, beginning with "Dearest Fritzie" and concluding with an homage of love. Throughout the period of our correspondence she worked as an investigator for the Congressional committees on the mobilization of manpower and industrial resources.

For my part, the frequent v-mail communicated my loneliness. "Time passes washing, eating, and keeping warm. I am just getting settled — rather too comfortably — before a successful fire. For the moment, it is too good, so I expect to get going soon. I saw the sun today. A tough little people, the English, but the American invasion will leave quite a dent."

The final letter from England is postmarked December 19, 1944. The next letter — my address changed from "somewhere in England" to "somewhere" — had an almost wistful tone. "What are you eating and wearing? What are you drinking? What are you doing? Has everyone forgotten about me already? Wear your white nightgown for me tonight."

Two weeks later I was in Paris during the opening of the Rundstedt offensive and the real show began for me.

I

## BAPTISM OF FIRE

**B**Y CHRISTMAS EVE 1944 the German offensive through the Ardennes had penetrated almost sixty miles beyond the Allied front lines, creating a salient six miles wide. Rundstedt's surprise attack in mid-December had turned Paris into a hotbed of wild rumors. Stories circulated that German spies were being dropped into the city by parachute. Anyone with a German accent became suspect, and foreign-born members of

Allied prisoner-of-war interrogation teams were frequent targets of mistrust. But boys in uniform will play, and some of our officers were picked up and hustled off to centers where their comrades, straightfaced, subjected them to questioning and practiced their clumsy techniques for hours on end, while the victims sweated it out, bewildered by their seemingly earnest erstwhile friends.

I was among the new American arrivals from England and was quartered in the elegant suburb of Le Vésinet, where streets led off in diverse directions from a roundabout with a bronze stag in the middle of a small plot of grass. Rail service to Paris was frequent; returning tipsy late at night I had only to follow one of the streets that branched off from the stag to reach my billet. But from which part of the stag — that was the question.

On December 22, still ignorant of the enormity of the German Bulge, which cost us seventy thousand casualties before it was rolled back, I had written to my wife: "Some sort of game is on . . . France is not what it seems like in the States. It is hard to communicate the furtive glances. It may be said that many Frenchmen prefer our occupation to the German. The tenor is Directoire. As far as the real show, one has a feeling of being swallowed up in something vast and Germanic in its enormity. Anyway, I did get here when they needed me most." The next day I was told that I was being attached to a newly formed Twenty-first Corps soon moving into action. "I have eaten in an officers' mess in Paris," I reported home, "and now I understand why those who have it hot and cold hate the *embusqués,* the guys holed up far behind the front. As under the Directorate, for him who has the paper, everything is available — which was not necessarily so in England. The honeymoon of liberation has not endured for long. I am having my last elegant meals with some indifference. It would have been good to carry away images of a city you felt had some living force behind it, rather than the spectacle of women perched on high-heeled wooden shoes and crowned with two-foot Directoire coiffures dyed blonde."

On the twenty-sixth I characterized as "gay-sad" my Christmas in Paris. "I had excellent drinks — in all a rather grotesque background for the real show, which ought to be coming on any time now. The cold is preferable to the English rain, but when there is nothing to burn except for Louis xv fauteuils you freeze. There is a story that the rooms where I am quartered were once occupied by Field Marshal Rommel. It feels peculiar to lie in a canopied bed where a German officer slept, with good cold air rushing in through the broken window." Before the year was out my mood changed. "Paris has been rather pleasant, at least there is plenty of cognac and good wine. The world is compressed for me from now on out. I know little and have nothing to write about. Well, nothing for a few days now."

On New Year's Eve, I wrote again. "While waiting to have my jeep fixed I drop you a little note. Yesterday I had much bubbly water in Paris with some of the *embusqués*. Boy, it's a good life, really better than London if you have any rank. Everything is so remote and yet so near. Soon comes retribution for the easy time I've had for six months. Tomorrow a new year and a new life for me."

While I was amusing myself at the Moulin Rouge, I later learned, the American troops were suffering in the area around Bastogne in one of the worst European winters in years. Despite warning signals from our intelligence officers, we were caught unawares by twenty-five German divisions that the Wehrmacht had managed to assemble secretly. Hitler's last spasm bewildered the American command. We paid for our hubris in blood.

My interrogation team set out from Paris on New Year's Day 1945 in a jeep that dragged along a trailer in which a large, four-door filing cabinet, meant to be stuffed with interrogation reports, rode in solitary splendor. As soon as we came to a running brook, we lifted the cabinet out of its trailer and heaved it into the water. Having performed this act of emancipation from the clanking dinosaur, we proceeded to Baccarat, our first stop, where we dallied while officers bought cartons of crystal for shipment home. In my mind's eye I saw mountains of expensive glass shattered by enemy shells. Information about the Battle of Bastogne raging in the north was still murky, and we had no idea precisely where the front line was. The army kept us in reserve for a period, with nothing much to do except listen to local tales about the collaborators who had worked with the Germans when they controlled the area. We were not commissioned to arrest miscreants. If we had been, we would have had to incarcerate half of any town through which we moved — only we didn't know which half. On a clear day, watching an armada of our planes as they flew in formation toward Germany, I was convinced that the war would soon be over, a pleasant prospect. French refugees from the shifting border with Germany were not that sanguine.

Without much prior notice we were ordered to cross the Vosges Mountains in a snowstorm. I spent my first night in the field sleeping on the floor of a farmhouse amid a score of other Corps officers who snored in disunison. To sleep under all conditions is the mark of a hardened soldier, which I was not.

As it turned out, the Twenty-first Corps did not move in the direction of the Battle of the Bulge, but had been sent southward to the Seventh Army area in order to counter the Germans' "Operation Nordwind," designed to extend the perimeters of their Alsace pocket centered in Colmar. On January 13, the Twenty-first Corps became operational and assumed the defense of the left flank of the Seventh Army. It had been decided on high that the conquest of the lost province of Alsace would be commanded by the Free French under General Jean de Lattre de Tassigny. The First French Army opened an offensive to eliminate the pocket with two divisions, the Fourth Moroccan Mountain Division on the west and the Second Moroccan Infantry Division on the east; and on January 25, the Twenty-first Corps Headquarters and Headquarters Company were transferred to the command of the French Army, taking tactical control of a new zone between the French First and Second Corps. Our mission was to assist in the reduction of the Colmar pocket by attacking in the direction of Brisach.

The joint operation with our French allies instilled in me a lasting prejudice against all such common ventures. I spoke both French and German tolerably well, and became a useful jack-of-all-trades as long as we were under the orders of de Lattre. At a midnight session de Lattre presented to the officers of our Corps his plan for capturing Colmar, preceded by a rambling, long-winded exposition of the political and military situation in the various other European theaters. At first I translated his pompous speech sentence by sentence; but as my fellow officers showed increasingly visible signs of boredom and drowsiness I condensed my summaries of his remarks more and more until they were reduced to laconic phrases and then grunts. Somehow the irritation provoked by de Lattre was directed against me, his hapless mouthpiece. Finally he stopped and turned with a flourish to our Corps commander, General Milburn, a genial ex-football coach: "And what do you say, *mon général?*"To which de Lattre received a terse reply that freed the assemblage from his oratorical envelopment: "Tell him we'll be there."

Although the recovery of Alsace was a sideshow of the major war in the west after Bastogne, casualties were heavy. Nothing went right during the campaign for the Colmar pocket — a rather simple operation — and on more than one occasion the French and American troops, heading in opposite directions through somebody's foul-up, were stuck in a gridlock on a narrow, crooked Alsatian street. The French *goumiers* (North Africans), laughing hilariously, frolicked around the jeeps and tanks. During one such tie-up the Germans sent from across the Rhine a few planes that strafed the entangled columns. While it was permissible for ordinary soldiers to duck under the jeeps in which we were riding, I judged it to be conduct unbefitting an officer, and endured the ordeal as a hero in a state of fright. If the Germans had had any air power left, our snaking line of troops and equipment would have ended in a massacre. But despite the gamble of the Ardennes offensive, the Third Reich was collapsing.

Communication between the French and American forces had its comic moments. Our Corps once used "cotter key" as its code name, and since telephone connections were less than adequate, my yelling *"C'est* cotter key *qui parle"* was to no avail. In exasperation I began to spell out the letters of the incomprehensible object according to the accepted formula. This only compounded the bewilderment. In extremis, I improvised a spelling scheme of my own: "C *comme cul,* O *comme onanisme,* T *comme teton,* E *comme érection."* The sexual allusions enlightened my French counterpart, though clearly neither he nor I knew what a "cotter key" was. We were city boys.

When Colmar was captured from the Germans the interrogation team warned our general in vain against moving Corps headquarters into the city, since it was obvious that the enemy would have left behind spies who, speaking Alsatian German, had easy access to information and could transmit the precise location of our installations to artillery on the other side of the Rhine. On its own authority our team established itself at some distance from the city center, apart from Corps headquarters. We occupied a farm, where the housewife cooked up a delectable stew from the ingredients of our tins of K rations. The prisoners of war whom we dragged along with us were put under guard in closed rooms and everything was tranquil until nightfall. Then, once they were fed, their voices rang out lustily in patriotic songs. We worried whether our small contingent of military police would be able to restrain them if they should make a dash for it.

By that time I was beginning to feel the effect of the "pantherpiss" (Kirschwasser), and I went up on the roof to survey the area, now brilliantly illuminated by bombs bursting into Colmar and igniting fires. Transfixed, I watched the display and turned philosophical, ruminating on the madness of war, listening to the chorus of German prisoners, hoping that our guards would stay awake, secretly troubled lest the German artillery miss its target and hit our farmhouse instead. The next day, when we returned to Colmar headquarters, we found that the Germans had lobbed a bomb right into the war room, making the situation map look crazier than usual.

Telephone lines became so hopelessly intertwined that I was sent to deliver a message to the French command in person. As I approached, wading through a sea of mud, shells began falling all around us. My hand trembled when I lit a cigarette and I felt ashamed standing before the seasoned warriors of the Free French. To cover my embarrassment I tried to jest about the cache of French brandy we had discovered and consumed the night before, to account for my shakes and colossal hangover. I was not convincing.

The lunch to which I was invited by the French lasted a full three hours and provoked in me a flood of puritanical, self-righteous reflections. We who were fighting for the liberation of their country never indulged in such Lucullan feasts in the midst of battle. We deferred our debauches until after-hours, when the generous liquor allotments we had awarded ourselves encouraged staid majors and colonels to swing from chandeliers after swilling a concoction of champagne and gin. The special officer who had been deputed to transport cases of the stuff from Antwerp, an active Allied port since November, was awarded a Bronze Star for his bravery in defense of the potions that won us a citation.

After the elimination of the Colmar pocket I was quartered for a while in the house of a widow whose young son had been picked up by the Germans and shipped off she knew not where. "To die for the motherland is sad enough," she wept, "but to die for the enemy! And all the time they hated him and called him Frenchman. My *bubele,* my *kindele,* in the ss! Maybe you'll find him and send him home to me. Such a handsome *bubele;* here is his *stuhlele.*" The widow's beds were large and soft, there was plenty of Alsatian wine and Kirschwasser, but my virtue was not assailed. My German, never free of a Boston Yiddish accent, was close enough to the Alsatian dialect to make conversation easy. The daughter of the house confided to me that she wished the next time around the stork would deposit her somewhere deep in France or in the heart of Germany. Being shunted back and forth between the two countries had become unbearable. I promised to look for their *bubele* in the prisoner-of-war corral. He probably was killed on the eastern front.

Elimination of the Colmar pocket was as significant a political as a military venture. When the Twenty-eighth Division of the Twenty-first Corps had reached the edge of Colmar on February 2, it had been ordered to pause, allowing the tanks of the French First Armored Division to enter the city ahead of us, a bow to the political sensibilities of the Free French. The Corps and its interrogation team were relatively new to combat and my baptism of fire had occurred under de Lattre, who, along with Generals Patton and Montgomery, was among the most temperamental leaders with whom Eisenhower had to contend. But like a first love, the battle of Colmar taught me more about the modern profession of arms than I have learned since.

By February 8 the Twenty-first Corps had completed its mission and eight days later reverted to the control of the Seventh Army. On February 9 and 11 I could announce triumphantly to my wife: "By now it is public record that we have been in on the elimination of the Colmar pocket. As a mission it had much in its favor — plenty of Riesling, Sylvaner, and Kirsch. The towns are all stage-set imitations of the *Cabinet of Dr. Caligari,* and the miracle of supply consists in the passage of two-way traffic up and down the narrow streets, without crashing into a house. A number of towns were smashed like those in Normandy; others got off more lightly.

"The warriors are sitting in their tents recuperating from the hardships of battle. The tents happen to have featherbed covers; the Boche got out too quickly to destroy all the wine cellars; we have the services of a pretty good cook; and we endure the boredom of each other's company. Walking up and down the former Adolf Hitler Street is our principal Colmar diversion."

On February 28 the Seventh Army under General Patch was regrouped: the Twenty-first Corps was placed on its left flank and we were ordered to hold the line abreast the Saar and the Moder. The plan was to mop up the Rhine-Palatinate area, destroy the pillboxes of the West Wall, cross the Rhine near Worms, and begin our drive into the German interior, moving southeast and due south to the Alps. We reached Weilheim and Bad Tölz in a rapid advance and occupied the whole of the southern front. On April 30 Hitler committed suicide, followed on May 6 by the surrender of German Army Group G under Field Marshal Kesselring. The next day, what was left of the German High Command signed the surrender of their army at Rheims. Instead of dashing to Berlin, which by arrangement was left to the Russians, we were ordered to Leipzig, scene of the last of my exploits.

# 2

## DISORDER OF BATTLE

THE FRENCHMEN CAME from across the Rhine, resplendent with the red fez and the beret, in liberated Hispana Suizas and Opels distributed according to rank, the conquered reconquering. To Frenchmen fornication did not involve fraternization, prohibited by Eisenhower; *goumiers* and Berbers for Brunhilde would solve the race problem, and there would arise a generation of little Africans to shame the purity of German blood.

The Americans dashed from the northwest, a rolling assembly line of jeeps, tanks, and trucks, keeping dates and appointed hours at Schweinfurt and Würzberg and Bamberg and Augsburg and Nuremberg and Munich. The offensive rumbled on with the fatality of night and day. It had all been planned in offices months, even years, before. It did not seem subject to the hazards of war. After the seizure of the Remagen Bridge the Germans rarely saw an American soldier marching. From Detroit to Nuremberg just one conveyor belt, and it whipped the Boche.

The English and the Canadians (with time out for tea) spread fanlike in the north, planting themselves on the seacoast from which they had been driven five years before, the humiliation of Dunkirk avenged.

The Russians poured in from the east and the southeast, less punctilious in timing, throttles open on steamrollers, arousing terror among the once mighty who had inflicted savage wounds with indifference.

The Fatherland was one vast battlefield. Dead lay unburied in the forests. As the snow melted, horses with *penes erecti* were uncovered; they looked like toppled painted figures from a merry-go-round. Rubble smoked in the cities. Boxcars from every ravished country in Fortress Europe stalled in marshaling yards and at railroad junctions. Fighter aircraft by Messerschmitt and Dornier and Focke-Wulf, without gas, were marooned along the four-lane superhighways that crisscrossed the Reich, sentinels of defeat camouflaged in the underbrush.

The u.s. Air Force, unmolested by a grounded Luftwaffe, were bombing and strafing at will. Any real or rumored concentration of men or weapons had become a target. Whatever stuck its head out of a foxhole or a trench drew artillery fire or a peppering from a P-38. Beneath a ceaseless shower of artillery and the never-ending alarms of bombers and fighters, the German soldier felt helpless; the enemy was toying with him, making sport. The American observer's Piper Cub, coasting for hours over the German lines without interference, seemed to direct every shell straight at him. Old-fashioned artillery was still a terrible morale breaker.

For months nothing had budged by day without the risk of a strafing. Throughout the night the German grenadiers had been forced to march in the darkness of the forest; no sooner had they been allowed to throw themselves down under a clump of trees than they were ambushed by motorized Yanks who had eaten a hearty breakfast. Supplies were heaped up in one German ration dump where there were no troops, while men were famished in another where the battle area had been interdicted by planes that pinpointed with precision and knocked out key bridges. The movement and countermovement of German troops had come to resemble the parading soldiers' chorus in a provincial operatic performance of *Faust,* the same handful appearing from behind the stage scenery and then disappearing again and again.

The Reich's economic chain unwound with the relentlessness of Greek drama. Since there were no railway carloadings there was no coal. No coal meant no gasoline. No gasoline meant no electric power. No power meant no production. Every doctor of economics in the Speer ministry could writhe, every engineer and technician shuffle his charts, every industrialist wriggle for priorities, and Hitler could rant at all of them — there was no reversing the downward spiral. They could corral their foreign slaves and rebuild their bombed plants; they could hide the factories in the forests and bury them deeper underground; but as long as the trails of transport had to wend their visible way over the surface of the earth they were targets of opportunity for American fighters and bombers.

Oil, the lifeblood of movement, was running dry. The attrition of the railway system forced the Germans to resort to circuitous motor hauls at the very time when they had no motor parts and the Allied bombers had complete mastery of the system of oil depots. There was no Luftwaffe in the air, no moving train on the ground, nothing but antiquated motor transport — a vehicular Babel from every occupied country in Europe — and stolen horses and oxen. The Germans wrangled among themselves for each liter of gasoline. Tanks on the way to battle were stalled on city streets and tankers had to threaten with their pistols Nazi Party big shots to get their fill at the expense of official vehicles. Headquarters monopolized the total monthly allotment of gasoline for a division, the equivalent of a GI's joyride in a jeep; the generals had to be mobile.

The towns and villages of South Germany were crowded with headquarters staffs of divisions and corps and armies, army groups and service commands, and special unattached units. The divisions had shrunk to company size; the companies under them had disappeared. "Colonel, go forward and pick up some accursed stragglers and we will be a division again. We have the maps and the requisite staff officers, a G-1, a G-2, and a G-3. There is still a war on!" But the colonel found other colonels from rival division staffs out in the field ahead of him on the same mission, and there was an internecine struggle among the division generals for the remnants.

"What *will* the Americans say, I thought to myself, if they capture me, me known as the Terror of Smolensk, Liège, and

Colmar, Generalleutnant Ralph, Count von Oriola, related to the royal houses of Sweden, Italy, and Czar Nicholas, without a man in the field! At least let me have the same number of men in the field as I have in headquarters. I gave orders: 'Go to all the towns and villages and gather up the stragglers. Let headquarters contribute the clerks; to hell with the War Diary. The clerks will give the division body. We have the maps.' The damned 17th ss Panzer Division. They had no right to go stealing our stragglers. I can prove it. Look here. They were ours in this area as shown by this map which draws the divisional boundary line sse from Dillingen. We'll live in tents, I said, we'll fight until the last bottle of brandy — horrible stuff, this Branntwein. Your whiskey is better. But keep the boots shiny, boy, I told my orderly; at any moment the Americans may come for our surrender."

O Clausewitz, what's the relevant chapter in your treatise on *Convergence of Attack and Divergence of Defense* for the German infantry lieutenant caught in a conflict of fleeing horse carts versus grinding tanks? He had just arrived fresh from the Officers Replacement Depot West and it was his first command. For him they threw together the butcher and the baker and the infantryman's jinx, the grounded air force boys who had never fired a shot. They gave them Panzerfausts (light bazookas) with promises of badges if they destroyed a tank and distributed a few rifles with promises of medals if they destroyed a plane. "Who said you cannot shoot down a plane with a rifle?" ran an official Order of the Day, "Courage! Courage! It has been done and the heroes have been awarded the Iron Cross by the Führer personally."

The lieutenant's Alarm Company was soon devoured. At the last moment he took himself off, made his way to a replacement station in the field, drew another Alarm Company with or without ammunition, returned to a position, served up his new Alarm Company to the enemy, and withdrew to repeat the process until he was captured. And then his eyes popped at the abundance of American tanks, trucks, jeeps, guns, and planes glistening in the sun.

"Why did you continue to send these boys into the fire when it was hopeless? Why did you lend yourself to this senseless slaughter?" I asked with the fatuous moral superiority of the victor.

"On my honor as a German officer, I really could not endure it any longer. My conscience plagued me day and night. I sought refuge in a confessional box and asked the chaplain about my responsibility. 'O father, shall I continue to send these boys to their death when I know that it is futile? I do not believe anymore.' And the priest defined my duty. 'My son, don't you remember the rules? Just obey. You are not responsible. It is not for you to determine. It is for you to obey and in turn to be obeyed and so turn the wheels of obedience that there may be order and light and darkness and a world. Responsibility rests with your superior and his superior and so on through channels until the highest. Go, my child, with an easy heart and fire your weapon in clear conscience, for in the eyes of the Judge you are blameless.' And so it was. I had my honor, my conscience, my obedience, and my salvation. Now my duty is done."

A lighthearted Austrian lieutenant who had aspired to be an actor on the Viennese stage was more ambivalent. "I went scouting in search of the new division to which I had been assigned and wherever I landed they stamped my papers and sent me on, a wanderer behind the lines, a wearer of the Iron Cross, second class, seeking the 347th Division through the Black Forest. 'O where, under what tree, can Lieutenant General von Hagl be hiding tonight?' I wondered. My papers have always been in order. See the stamps at the control points. I'm no deserter. I was looking for my vanished division, and the intelligence services of two armies, so I see, did not know where it had dug in. Should I tell you that perhaps I did not look too hard, as I fed on the peasant's eggs and pinched his daughter's rump? It is dishonorable to desert, but maybe not against the rules of the Old Fritz to hold the line until they come and get you."

The chain of command depended on lines of communication and these were shattered. They had no telephone wires for field armies except the internal network of the Reich, regularly disrupted by Allied terror attacks. And when we captured a local telephone system intact, there was Jovian fun in plugging in and barking orders at random all over Germany. Radio circuits were unreliable since friend and foe could intercept anything; the Germans had to resort to messengers on motorcycles without gas. The resulting order of battle brought administrative chaos and drove the strict military housekeepers to distraction.

In April the German High Command began to bunch the 13s on the American Seventh Army front. They lined up the 13th Army Corps on the flank of the 13th ss Panzer Corps and threw them both into the 13th Service Command area and formed a new unit called the 13th Panzer Group (without panzers) and then sent replacements and special orders to all of them. "On penalty of death report to the co of the 13th." But which 13th and where was it? They confused and deceived their enemy all right. "But what about us? What a humiliation for me, General of the Waffen ss, when you ask me what is on my right flank and what is on my left flank and I do not know. Honestly, on my word of honor as an officer, I do not know."

One night Captain Klein received eight different orders from eight different higher commands, each claiming him as their very own. If he obeyed any one of them he still had seven court-martials to face. Major Schnake was a last-ditch man. He fortified the hills to the north of a town with machine guns. Two 88mm guns, the German weapon of choice, were moved about with horses until the horses collapsed. A few shots were fired into the town from which they had just been driven; then the guns were dragged by sweating cannoneers to fire a few rounds into another town. Mobile defense.

The forward observer of a German artillery unit was picked up dozing in an abandoned bus. He had called the shots back to his battery but nobody answered and he went to sleep. There were at least two dummy artillery positions for each real piece, to deceive our reconnaissance planes. Soon there were only dummy artillery positions. Brigadier General Sessner had a rocket brigade of 300mm "screaming meemies" and he lay in an observation post watching the Sherman tanks roll by. He could have blown them to smithereens, except that he had received no ammo. A brigade of new 300mm multi-barreled rockets lacked anything to feed on. King Tigers, the new monster German tanks, had to be dug into fixed positions in the earth because there was no gas. Everywhere there were Panzerfausts, the people's weapon. They had manufactured 15 million pieces in December 1944 and distributed them to the civilian Volksstürm throughout the Reich. But the people were afraid of their weapon. They pulled out the charges and went to battle with empty shells. It was safer that way. A few were left in the gutters of the village square and they tore curious German children to pieces.

During the siege of a city, defending a house was the best deal for the grenadiers who had a snout full. They simply hid in the cellar and waited. The lieutenant who was their CO could not hunt down every last group. They were forgotten until the Americans came. What were they expected to do, fight against Shermans? (Everything on wheels was called a Sherman tank by then.) Getting chow was hard in a cellar and they didn't want to send an emissary to the company mess; it was too dangerous to maintain contact. They had starved before. As soon as they were captured the pleading began: "We haven't eaten for three days." For some reason it was always three days. "Thank God, everything is over now. It's an awful feeling to get killed in the last days of a war."

Toward the end, staying put in the forest was pretty safe. Some farmers drove the soldiers away; others let them sleep in the barn; a few even gave them something to eat. Bavarian peasants who had never known the bite of war treated the defenders of their expanding and contracting Reich like stray dogs. In thousands of German wallets were carefully preserved safe conduct passes for deserters, signed in due form by General Eisenhower, which had been shot over in artillery shells and dropped from planes. These Germans were hedging. The little grenadier was forever plotting desertion, but desertion is more easily thought than done.

The deep hatred of the front-line infantrymen for the staff generals and the sheltered ones back home smoldered in the bosoms of the abandoned soldiers. They were being sacrificed for something they no longer understood, only to give the Party Bonzen (big shots) another short-term lease on life. Everything had lost its meaning except getting out alive and returning to Hilde and the kids. The German family survived the wreckage despite casual fornication. Tears flowed as fathers told of sons killed on the eastern front. This was the second war as privates for these men of forty-five. What had they been good for? Fillings for the teeth of the Siegfried line, where they had lain in damp bunkers complaining to each other of their aches and pains. They were a nuisance to the vanquished and to the victors.

Kids of fifteen in uniform could be hard as rock. Kids of fifteen could whine that they wanted to go home to mama. Weeping children and sniveling old men were among the last defenders of the Reich. And the kids took a few potshots at us after it was all over. Just for good measure. To remind us that the younger generation was still around.

In the last days a substantial portion of the Wehrmacht took off and went home. They retreated and retreated until they backed into the yard of a wife or a girlfriend or a relative. In the forests lay heaps of Wehrmacht and ss uniforms. The armed forces disappeared into civvies and nobody much cared.

"Let 'em go," snarled the American MP, "We've got too many mouths to feed as it is."

"Take me, I'm a prisoner," pleaded the limping warrior, who wore the *edelweiss* of a mountaineer.

"The hell I will! Fifteen kilometers down the road you'll find a cage. Go lock yourself up."

Others stripped to the waist, made pilgrims' staffs from the broken limbs of the trees, and trudged home, even hundreds of miles. The hobnailed boots that had mashed every nation in Europe were now carrying back the bronzed, sweaty bodies of the defeated heroes. Or a gang would get together, find a dilapidated Wehrmacht vehicle that ran on wood, pile in the girls — there were almost always girls — and move on. It broke down; they fixed it; it broke down again. They had plenty of time. They huffed and puffed and blew the dirty smoke into clean American nostrils.

*In der Heimat, in der Heimat,*
*Gibt es ein Wiedersehn.*

In the homeland, in the homeland,
There we'll meet again.

It was a matter of accident, depending on the zeal of the local Allied command, whether anybody bothered pulling them into a POW enclosure or let them roam about the countryside. Some roads were crowded with truckloads of prisoners, forty and fifty truckloads at a time driven along the autobahns. Villagers passed bread out to them. Women waved; the prisoners did not often wave back. They were poured into open fields, a hundred thousand to a field, guarded by a few machine guns and spotlights, a swarm of milling creatures. Theoretically, the whole male population of Germany between the ages of sixteen and forty-five who were not disabled were POWs. In the mass they stank.

"Just three kilometers from home. Caught just three kilometers from home. I almost made it, pushing through the American lines after we fled back across the Rhine. And now I'll probably never see my children again. Want to look at their pictures?" The German POW kept his whole life in a wallet, leaving nothing to the imagination. Here is the Frau Else and two blond children playing in the garden. There a flabby Frenchwoman, naked except for her black stockings, memory of the days. Feelthy pictures. Two Polish women. Female heads from Italy and Czechoslovakia and leave in Pomerania. The Place de la Concorde. Two or three hanging peasant bodies from Poland or the Ukraine. An obituary about Hans from the *Rothenburger Anzeiger*. A bit of string. Letters from Else describing the bombings. Letters from Hedda on lost love after all the cigarettes and chocolates she had sent him. And the diary for the American intelligence officer. They had marched 1,700 miles and the place-names en route were meticulously recorded. Then a combination knife, spoon, and fork, and scraps of old newspaper, containing no secrets, just to use for shitting.

"We know. You'll either kill us or turn us over to the Russians. That is what Roosevelt and Stalin decided at Yalta."

"Which would you prefer?"

"It's all the same to me now. I've lost everything. If only I could have seen my wife once more. When can I write a letter? If I could see my wife for one hour, on my word of honor as a German officer I would come back. Where should I run to?"

The egotistical rabbits. Didn't they think other people wanted to see their wives too?

One POW expected special treatment by virtue of being the son-in-law of Hans Dieckhoff, the former German Consul General in New York. Another was a salesman for I.G. Farben and imagined we would be interested. There was an archaeologist who had worked with an American professor. A half-Jew required the judgment of Solomon to be meted out: one half detained, the other half liberated. They always needed to urinate and defecate and drink water and eat. Their papers had been forgotten two echelons down. Somebody had stolen their watch.

Prisoners kept piling into the appointed fields from every regular and irregular unit the German General Staff had ever conceived. A batch of a thousand prisoners yielded two hundred and fifteen separate unit identifications: the 236th Fortress Engineer BN, the 64th Marine Regiment, the 136th AA, the 12th Horse Groomers Unit, the 386th Coastal Battery Guards, the 224th Rocket Brigade, ZBV (for special purposes), the 16th Light Div. SS Germania, the 9th PZ Division, the 6th Mtn. Div. Hq. Troop, 13th Service Command. One division had cannibalized another and then in turn been cannibalized. The Wehrmacht ended as a military hash. For the formal surrender there was an order of battle, with army groups, armies, corps, and divisions, but that was as much a shell of reality as the facades of the bombed German buildings.

Only in one sphere was the German administrative triumph uneclipsed, the universe of files and paper forms. Each headquarters carted along the record of every act of company punishment since the inception of the Polish campaign. In retreat, orders were to save the papers first, for in the beginning was the word. Bombs may destroy lives but what chaos when they destroy papers! No paybook, no pass, no record of civilian occupation, no ration card. Then the administrative order is muddled and the tentacles of control are loosened. Jews with a tuft of blond hair, escapees from bombed-out work camps, can pass themselves off as Volga Germans despite a heavy Minsk accent and wander about with impunity gathering up secrets for the enemy. Take away a German's papers and he is cut off from the world, a waif. German soldiers with pockets full of papers clogged the highways. Papers for every occasion: for being caught by the ss and for being nabbed by the field police; a few old and tattered Social Democrat party books for the Americans; papers for being late on furlough; and papers for no purpose. And when the jig was up there were more papers: hundreds of thousands of soldiers and clerks typed discharge papers for one another dated from the end of April through May 8.

"Me of the Wehrmacht? Look at my discharge papers, provisionary to be sure but you understand, communications with the central Adjutant General's Department are at the moment so to speak inadequate. Hence my Adjutant General said, 'General, we must improvise. I write you your dismissal. You write me mine.' Under field conditions an officer must use his initiative."

The war was over and they dismissed each other individually

and collectively and headed for home, at peace with the world and with a paper of honorable discharge. To fool the Americans? Gods no! For pensions, so that they could collect disability insurance and establish their rights and privileges under the orders of the Reich — to enjoy the emoluments of veterans of six years of hard war.

"You, where are your papers?"

"Here, Herr Captain, my papers are in order. When do I get paid next? When do I collect for my extra children? Please, my papers."

And then came confusion and they gave Fritz the papers of Karl and Karl the papers of Johann and Johann the papers of Sigismund. What was Sigismund with the papers of Ethelbert? Was he Sigismund or had he become Ethelbert? Papers make the German man.

After the Americans met up with the Russians at Torgau on April 25, the situation map in the u.s. War Room resembled a Dali fantasy — drooping front-line boundaries and protrusions here and there fashioned grotesque objects. The temper of resistance among the Germans varied, depending upon the quality of the stragglers and the character of the local German commander, his age, state of health, and degree of participation in the code of obedience. In many areas German troops made frantic attempts to surrender to American units in order to avoid falling into the hands of the dreaded Russians.

But when a fellow like Sturmbannführer Dirnagel of the Waffen ss got control of a sector, as he did around Bad Mergentheim, regular Wehrmacht superiors in higher echelons might just as well have filed away in their field cabinets all seven copies of any orders they presumed to send him. He derived his powers directly from Himmler and was fighting his own war. "Men of the Waffen ss, to the mountains!" They could hide and live on mountain flowers, blue flowers, in the loneliness of the forest. Food had been stored away for months. A few weeks before the formal surrender, ss troops had come through Bavarian towns at the foot of the Alps, picked up their women, and gone into the mountains. There must have been a lot of hot loving in those last days. And when they were finally flushed out, the women — true Germania — wept copiously and insisted upon trailing along into captivity.

During the last stages of the war the ss had established a new order of battle for the German army, one that could not be studied in any of the official manuals. *Most forward echelon:* the men of the stomach battalions (or the duodenal battalions, as British Intelligence insisted, finding distasteful the German colloquialism for these mobilized ulcerated men). The ulcerated ones were expendable and were commanded to hold until the last ulcer burst. *Second echelon:* directly behind the stomach battalions, the stragglers of the regular army whom the roving ss Field Police had picked up — air force boys who had spent recent months polishing ack-ack equipment for Goering when they should have been learning to creep and crawl with a Panzerfaust, navy boys on trains wrecked en route to Kiel, artillery boys for whom the infantry had always been something to cover, wretched headquarters clerks who had scribbled their way through five and six years of war never doubting that a pen offered more longevity for its manipulator than a K-98, cooks, medics, signal units who as specialists had resisted all attempts to be sacrificed in the infantry. *Third echelon:* behind the stomach battalions and the strays, stood the ss, guns loaded. Stomach-ulcer boys and the cooks who gave them the ulcers were deployed against columns of Sherman tanks. The ss stayed behind and promised to hang them if they came back alive or only slightly wounded. The ss were to be preserved for the end, perhaps for that which was to be after the end.

ss men had their blood types tattooed under their arms, at least they were supposed to (though sometimes the tattooing system broke down). They were the doomed, for the conquered nations of Europe had sharp recollections of their propensities in former days of victory. But what was left of the ss was not the glory of German manhood, long since pushing up daisies. A hodgepodge from every occupied country in Europe, the willing and the unwilling, they bore distinguished names — Götz von Berlichingen, Gross Deutschland, Prinz Eugen, Viking, Germania. ss divisions that had once struck terror throughout Europe now became the coveralls for the impressed inferior races over whom Superman had ruled, the Volksdeutsche (folk Germans). Only the noncoms and the officers were Aryan Germans of good stock. The other ss remnants had to bear on their heads the blood vengeance stored up for those pure Germans who had preceded them under the same banners. Allied front-line troops did not load themselves down with too many ss prisoners.

The ss were supposed to be the tough boys, and some were, but in captivity they looked rather funny in their special hooded camouflage uniforms of dappled-leaf colors. They had the appearance of tailless cats. This horde from the conquered nations had been subjected to political and racial training.

"What did you learn about races, peasant idiot from Lithuania?"

"I learned . . . I learned that there are black races and white races and that you can tell by looking at people to what race they belong."

"And you believe in the Führer?"

"Yes."

"And you are ready to die?"

"Yes."

"And you want to die?"

"No."

"And you, Dutchman, why did you join that traitor Mussert?"

"Because I had to or lose my job or go to a concentration camp."

"And you?"

"I'm Hungarian. They took me away from my horses."

"And you?"

"I'm of the Shqipetari."

"The what?"

"Albanian, formerly of ss Scanderbeg."

The ss Viking had been marched all the way from Finland, the ss Germania had been shipped from Norway. The ss Viking had been promised a furlough when they reached their home station in Ellwangen, but instead they were chosen to be the last defenders of the Reich.

"The ss man's life had not been a bad one," said the shoemaker in Ellwangen. "Every Saturday night the village had to contribute a quota of girls to the dance at the Replacement Training Center. I always said my daughter was sick. But then the Gauleiter called me and said, 'Well?' and I said, 'I contribute to Winter Relief,' and he said 'Your daughter,' and I said, 'She is sick,' and he said, 'She will be!'"

Now the ss troops of impressed Volksdeutsche were intimidated by their commanders: it was Siberia or death or worse if they were captured. "Tell them what they did to you," urged the political officer, displaying his specimen of an escaped ss prisoner of war at the orientation lecture to the raw Volksdeutsche troop. "You know what it means to be sent to Russia

— Murmansk, the salt mines, endless whippings. Finally, they dig holes, bury your body up to the neck, and then have a regiment march over your head. Only by a miracle did I escape." With that morale booster under their belts, the ss either became the desperadoes of the countryside or vanished among the surrounding yokels, tearing the skulls and bones off their uniforms, dressing in anything they could get hold of to avoid detection. Why should they be singled out? But there was that telltale tattoo on the underarm. Not all the waters of the Danube could wash it away.

In the end the newborn ss were fed up. They began to disbelieve the horror descriptions of their impending fate if taken prisoner. "It is better to remain alive. So we'll work. For five years, ten years, and then it will be over. What can be bad now? Give me food and I work. You are doing the ss a grave injustice. Today the ss is no longer what it used to be. Anybody on two feet is part of the ss. The Replacement Center sent so many to the ss and so many to the army. Nobody asked me whether I wanted to be ss." And he was speaking the truth, after his fashion. There were military ss and general ss who guarded concentration camps and ss who were just traffic cops. Once I stayed awake half the night waiting to interrogate a contingent of ss officers. When I saw the first officer with "ss Galicia" on his sleeve I burst into uproarious laughter. In the Boston ghetto where I was born a Galician Jew was the butt of ridicule. Was this frightened creature the monster for whom I had screwed my face into a terrifying grimace?

# 3

## WAITING FOR THE AMERICANS

**O**N THE 24TH OF FEBRUARY, 1945, Hitler assembled the leaders of the forty-two Gaus of the Reich in the Great Hall of the Chancellery in Berlin. For once, the Deputy Leader of the Party, Martin Bormann, did not kick them in their spreading rumps before and after their admission into the presence. They were there to commemorate the Day of the Founding Fathers. On this occasion the heads of the Party did not have to vie with bedecked and betailored generals for attention. They were the Kingdom once again and he was their Führer come to speak to them in the hour of need, while the Americans and the English were prodding the body of the Reich from the west, banging away at the Siegfried armor, probing for the weak links in the mail, still wondering what sort of hide lay beneath. Was it blubber or was it more mail?

Gauleiters were old comrades in arms and vice. They knew their districts from eating and drinking with their people, but they dared not speak, for in Berlin who knew whom and anyway who would listen? It was indiscreet to repeat the pernicious anecdotes overheard in streetcars and amid the rubble on the morrow of a terror bombing. Even gold-button officials had been executed for defeatism. They were all forced into a conspiracy of silence. One-armed Max Amann, Hitler's sergeant in the First Infantry Regiment of Bavaria in World War I, had heard more than was good for him in his bailiwick in Munich, the birthplace of the movement and its graveyard. His Bavarians would not stay in line. His loquacious, heart-on-their-tongue Bavarians could no more not talk than not drink their beer, watery though it was. Bormann had sent a Westphalian party leader into Bavaria to tighten the reins. Amann had tried to protest to his Führer in person but Bormann would never let him in for a private interview. He would counter every request for an audience with a blunt "Is it something pleasant or something unpleasant?" And since it was admittedly unpleasant, Amann stayed out. He had come to the Gauleiters' meeting in the Chancellery with the firm resolve to corner the Führer and speak his mind. A Westphalian party leader in Bavaria — what an outrage!

In the meantime Hitler orated as usual, beginning in the beginning, evoking the early struggles of the movement. He used notes, which the Gauleiters considered peculiar. Hitler's head was shaking and his hand was trembling and he drew their attention to his pains and unsteadiness: "My hands may quiver but my heart remains firm and my head remains cool!"

He reviewed the statistical evidence on the state of the war and sneered at the numbers that foretold defeat. As if war were merely a computation of tanks and planes! Men would then never begin to fight. They would only use an adding machine to calculate the war utensils of their adversaries and if outnumbered would surrender. Had the movement been built on arithmetic it would not have emerged from the beer cellar. Courage is still the force of men. Courage and faith in the secret. They could not know the mystery weapon, for to know it before it was born was to know the secret of life and death. But they had to have faith in the womb of the Kingdom and in the men of science who had forged a v-1 and a v-2 and a Vengeance-to-come. The ordinary people back home must be made to hold out unto the end, because as long as one German in the bowels of an underground laboratory or factory was racking his brain, he might yet bring them revenge for Churchill's victory.

The cauldron was simmering and all the fires of hell were concentrated to give it heat, but time could not be bought. If Hitler had only had another moment of time, if his mad scientists had only thought faster, if Sprit could be made from spittle — he would have had it, the new weapon that was mocked by Germans who had stopped believing.

*Lieb Vaterland machst ruhig sein,*
*Mann zieht schon jetzt die Oma ein;*
*Kann das die neue Waffen sein?*

Dear Fatherland, you may rest secure,
Granny's already being enlisted;
Can that be the new weapon?


Why not believe? Vengeance 2 had been launched as the Führer had promised. He never lied. "I assure you that before the end of the month," the clubfooted one had whispered among the assembled. But the month had no end; it stopped short and Goebbels lied for the last time.

And the Gauleiters left the Chancellery with renewed zeal. They believed again. Perhaps not all of them. Frick, former Minister of the Interior, Protector of Bohemia and Moravia, the man who fitted murder and arson into the Weimar Constitution, was already possessed with doubt and it made him look mousey. But the run-of-the-mill Gauleiter went back to his district to distribute the thousand favors and make the petty exceptions in the laws upon which states are built.

The people in the towns of neat manure piles and cows pleaded, "Soldier, go away from my door! Go defend Ansbach or Ochsenfurt, but go, do not defend us. We want our barns and our cattle. Woe unto us if you defend us! We are ready with white cloths, neat and well washed to make a good impression with our cleanliness. We have handkerchiefs and tablecloths, pillowcases and sheets, great sheets, for there is grandeur even in surrender. Weapons of war are farsighted these days. Maybe Tante Hedwig's petticoats will do. Maybe two of them would be better: one from the roof and one from the window; one if they come from the north and one if they come from the south." But the Gestapo and the ss were hanging those who displayed white flags. The battle rarely seesawed, but when it did, the ss boys carried out what the orders said. Who dared surrender and see himself dangling at the crossroads?

Old Party fights that for years had secretly rankled broke out in the cities and hamlets. Nazis were really political dualists in their administration despite the much ballyhooed "One Führer, One Reich, One People." Only German émigrés who had paper to waste wrote books and memoranda depicting them as monists and their regime as a monolith. Nazis were not the state. As they learned from Lenin, that would have destroyed the revolutionary momentum of their movement. They were the Party, parallel to the state at every functional level, yet not the state. In their jargon they were the male, the seminal; the state, or the nation, was the female, ever being conquered and aroused for action. The Bürgermeister of a town, the old dotard, was *of* the Nazis, but not always *the* Nazi. The Ortsgruppenleiter (district Party group leader) was the Party and he controlled the municipality through, against, or with the old mayor, who retained as many of the decorations and trappings of the medieval burg as tradition and architecture and Party would allow. In the conduct of everyday affairs the reverend mayor chafed in silence. He loved Hitler, children, his wife, his sons who had died for the Third Reich. But why did the Glorious Kingdom that was yet to be for a thousand years have to incarnate itself locally in the person of that scoundrel, that wastrel, Schulz the Ortsgruppenleiter? And the Ortsgruppenleiter knew that Herr Schmidt was a post-1933 Nazi selected for his age, as mayors are wont to be in patriarchal societies, an old-fashioned fool.

In the moment of the Reich's agony their ways parted. As the day of a town's siege approached, the Ortsgruppenleiter gathered the Volksstürm in the public square and exhorted them to fight for their yet unraped wives and yet unpillaged houses. He described the Judeo–Anglo–Saxon–Bolshevist conspiracy, embodied at the gates of their fair city in the Negroes and the Indians who led Americans into battle with primitive howls, to be followed in the second echelon by gangsters from Chicago. The Gauleiter invoked the Führer and the weapon that was to be.

When the Ortsgruppenleiter had finished his harangue, the Volksstürm gingerly went off to their roadblocks as ordered, and he to his Opel filled with the last gasoline in the area. Then he sped off toward the south or the east or in whatever direction the district leaders were fleeing. When the last Volksstürmer saw his leader save his skin before the echoes of the *Heils* had stopped reverberating from wall to wall, he thought of his warm bed and his Hilde and he quietly stole away. Better a live ass.

The Bürgermeister was abandoned by the Party. Besieged by men of property, he bethought himself of the medieval beauties of the town and the English and American tourists, not to speak of the Scandinavians, who in years gone by used to flock there to admire the moat and the square and the guild-hall. Did not a city father in a ruff go out to greet Wallenstein or Tilly and beg for mercy when the burghers had chosen the wrong side in the Thirty Years' War? Such burgomasters were immortalized in painting, revered by fellow townspeople long after kings and princes and generals were forgotten. He would parley. How the Nazis had deceived him! Never was a people so lied to and betrayed. He, the Bürgermeister, had only a puffing, wood-burning vehicle; the Ortsgruppenleiter had the gas. He, the mayor, would confront the enemy. After all, they were not Russians. Uncle Max was living in Milwaukee, and in 1938 the mayor had danced with a matron from Chicago. If they were Russians that would be different. The *hausfrauen* were on his side. They were pulling down the roadblocks and sending their menfolk to bed where they belonged. In the marketplace the women would intercede at the feet of the American general on a rolling tank as they did before Tilly on horseback and they would all be spared.

Commandant Colonel Körner of Ansbach summoned to a conference all the subcommandants from the surrounding defense area, along with the mayor and the bishop and the Gauleiter. To defend or not to defend. The orders said "to the last man." On the wall map they marked the main line of resistance around the town and then another line for the retreat after the main line of resistance had been breached. Lieutenant Seifert was ordered to blow up the bridges. The men of the town begged the lieutenant to spare their bridges, which led to the fields, for if there were no bridges, there would be no food. Colonel Körner disdained such considerations.

The political officer from higher headquarters made a speech. If the Führer wants to sacrifice Ansbach for a loftier purpose, he knows. In Berlin they need time and we can buy it for them. Traitors will be shot. Any soldier found eight kilometers behind the front line who cannot explain his presence will dangle. Any soldier captured who is not wounded will lose his German citizenship and his wife and children will be deprived of their ration tickets. Anybody in town who shows signs of defection will be dealt with summarily. "Ha! Ha!" thought Schliefer the orderly, "my wife is in Silesia being raped by the Russians. You can no longer scare me. I did not survive three Russian winters to die during the last days of the war."

The ss inspectors examined the bridges and were not satisfied with Lieutenant Seifert's demolition preparations. They posted a guard. There would be no repetition in Ansbach of the Remagen Bridge treachery. Suddenly as they were standing there the stone span exploded into the air along with the townspeople who had been sunning themselves. Back at the conference, the bishop pleaded for his church, the mayor for his city hall. Colonel Körner, with a glance at the political officer from higher headquarters, was adamant. Ansbach would allow itself to be destroyed.

When the political officer finally took off, the civil and military defenders of Ansbach brought out the drinks. The last of the Hennessy reserved for the Wehrmacht was to be consumed. They turned on Radio Luxembourg and looked at the map. Colonel Körner repeated a studied cynical remark appropriate to defeat. It was tacitly understood that each sub-commandant in the Ansbach district would act in accordance with his expedient conscience in the last days. After the drinks, Colonel Körner went out and approved the hanging of two boys of seventeen who had taken off when they should have died on the reverse slope of Hill 658.

"Victory or Siberia!" was smeared on the walls.

"What are the Americans like?"

"They are gangsters from Chicago forced into the army. They are led by two Jews, Baruch and Rosenfeld, who are avenging themselves for what we did to the Jews. They had to make war because of their unemployed. Capitalist countries have millions of unemployed. They go to war to kill off some of them."

"The white ones look human, but the black ones, they are monsters!"

Sergeant Steiner, a tanker, had written to his Helena, "I see them in my dreams at night. Great swarms of Shermans dashing down upon us with black men sticking out of the cockpits. It is terrifying and I wake up shrieking."

"Don't believe it. I have been to America. Americans are people, too."

"Let's put an end to it. We cannot stand the bombings any longer. Day and night. Hermann Goering said his name was

Schmul Meyer if they would ever be able to bomb our cities through his network of flak defenses. Well, his name is Schmul Meyer. Every night, every night sleeping in the cellar. Bombed out three times."

"We are the Flüchtlinge, the refugees, those who fled from the east and the west. In our own country we have to beg for charity. These Swabians are selfish. They have luxurious homes and crowd us into cellars and barracks. We were cleared out of the Saar area because of the Siegfried line and sent here for safety. But we get nothing to eat. We have ration coupons and they send us to the devil. They hog everything for themselves. The local people here who have never been through a real bombing like that of October 3 in Saarbrücken treat us like strangers. What has the war meant to them? They have their cows and their pigs."

When a spearhead of the American army had penetrated within twenty kilometers of a city, the rumblings of civil strife were heard openly in the streets. A surrender movement, which had been stealthily nurtured by a handful of Germans and an Allied agent or two, erupted. Americans were to be welcomed with the spectacle of German devouring German. There were plots and counterplots, the wily ones staying in the background, like old Von Epp in Munich. He had sent a young zealot to seize the radio station, but the surrender roared into the microphone was cut short by the crack of a pistol. Uprisings were usually premature and abortive. The Americans were proceeding according to plan and the little German Michel was too impatient.

A German field officer was regularly dispatched on a tour of those hamlets that did not merit elaborate paper defense plans to inspect the roadblocks and tank ditches on possible avenues of the American approach — primitive impediments in a war of tanks and planes. The officer understood the idiocy and pretense of these wooden barricades manned by decrepit Volksstürmers trying to repel with Panzerfausts — weapons that terrified only their own bearers — an invasion of fire-spitting tanks. But orders were orders. Every man to his duty.

And the women with wombs empty and wombs full knew theirs. They tore down the roadblocks and by the time the inspecting officer had reached the next town a pathway had been cleared for the Shermans. Come, Americans, and spare our town. But often the retreating ss got to the town before the Americans, shot a few traitors, and there was a rush to reconstruct the roadblocks.

Battle orders were constantly shifting as the jurisdictions of field armies and city defense commandants overlapped. Four commandants in as many days presided over the agony of Würzburg. Where surrender parleys miscarried, there did not seem to be much left that was worth saving after the American pre-attack air and artillery barrage. Some chose to die amid the rubble. While officers tried to guess the direction of the American main effort, Shermans and Grants appeared from everywhere. The German defense committee sat in their dugout with dead telephones and waited.

In the last hours before surrender, the good burghers to whom everything had been measured out for years went on a spree, ransacking their own warehouses. Faced with the reality of defeat, the army supply depots finally made legal a wholesale distribution of shoes and clothing. For a few wild hours the German Michels forgot themselves. Refugees from other parts of the land and the old residents fought with each other over their respective rights to the free booty of the Wehrmacht. Was it reserved for local inhabitants only or was it to be equally distributed among all men of German blood before the Americans came in and grabbed it? The squabbles of those last queues lived on after the formal surrender, and the wrongs of distributive justice were avenged in a torrent of denunciations to the American authorities.

Finally the hour had come for the besieged town. Snipers on the outskirts fired their last rounds. Flagwavers destroyed their swastikas and substituted the white of purity and surrender. Women strained in anticipation mingled with fear for a peek at the first invaders. Valuables had been hidden away in a hole dug in the garden or in the manure pile. The last rites had been performed. The conqueror found his enemy sweeping the debris of the bombings from the sidewalks. Children welcomed him with the v for Victory sign made with the index and middle finger à la Churchill.

4

# THE LITTLE MICHELS

IN 1936 GUSTAV SONDERHOF wanted the Jew Halperin's apartment and so he paid a consideration to Berthold, in charge of housing in the city of Leipzig. Halperin disappeared and Sonderhof had his apartment, but it annoyed him that he had to pay for what was his due by right of being an Aryan and having two sons in the Wehrmacht and one daughter a *Blitz Mädel* and another daughter a nurse. When the Americans came and hung out a sign with the enigmatic letters c.i.c., Sonderhof presented himself and made a deposition, and Berthold, who had in the meantime become anonymous, fell into the automatic arrest category and Sonderhof had his little revenge. From then on there was a haven for all who wanted to commit little spites and free themselves of the fixation of hate against the enemies that beset every man. Today you squeal on me, tomorrow I squeal on you. The Counterintelligence Corps heard the tales and recorded them.

Once they had told the Gestapo: "He was a defeatist. He listened to Radio Luxembourg. He laughed about the Führer. I overheard him tell the one about the last three stragglers — you know who they will be? Hitler, Himmler, and Goebbels." Then the squeal was turned. "He was a fanatical Nazi. He sent my brother to a concentration camp because he was a Social Democrat."

"And why did you send his brother to a concentration camp? Was that nice?"

"It was not me, I swear it was not me. I had to join the Party, all civil servants had to join the Party. I am not a confirmed Nazi. Ask my wife, Martha, she will tell you. My Party book dates from 1940. I was forced to join the Party to eat. Many is the time that the Ortsgruppenleiter called me before him and said, "Seidlitz, why is it that we do not see you at meetings?' And I answered, 'I am busy with my duties.' And he said, 'Your duties to the state come first.' I always knew they would be the ruin of Germany. If you are looking for a fanatical Nazi take Teschner, the one who has the wholesale potato house. And Greitz is an even more ardent Nazi than him."

"I am of the Party only since the edict of 1942. He wears the gold pin of a pre-1933 Party member. He is the real terror of this town. He was always upbraiding everybody and threatening them for not doing enough for Winter Relief. And how he bragged about his copy of *Mein Kampf* with Ley's signature in it! I am a quiet man, always stood on the sidelines, never pushed myself forward."

In a demonstration of German politics for the benefit of my colonel, I asked a bedraggled private plucked at random out of a batch of prisoners, "And you, what were you before Hitler? To which political party did you belong?"

"To none. I was a nonparty man. I was apolitical."

"Yes, but did you ever vote? Whom did you last vote for? What party?"

"Democratic."

"Social Democratic?"

"Jawohl."

"That means that you were sort of in favor of the Communists?"

"Jawohl."

"And as such for whom did you last vote for President?"

"Hindenburg."

"Ah."

"That is the political mind you must educate. Such confusions must be abolished. You must make them understand the differences between a Democrat and a Social Democrat, a Radical Socialist, a Centrist, a Christian Democrat, a Republican Christian, and a Communist and a Socialist, so that they can think for themselves," I pontificated half in jest.

"We don't want to have anything to do with politics," insisted little Michel, "We want bread and work. If only we had been satisfied after the defeat of France, how happy we could have been. If only we had had enough after we got the Ukraine, how happy we could have been. If only we had invaded England instead of Russia. As soon as America declared war, I said to myself, me an old soldier of 1914, it will be the same again. We are lost. But what could I do, I a little grenadier, a helpless one. They put me through the mill. Lie down! Get up! Lie down! Get up! In the mud, and then my uniform had to be spotless. How could I, a little fellow, desert? If I deserted they would kill my wife and children or take away their rations. I thought nothing about myself, but the little ones. If I deserted by day my officer would shoot me. If I deserted by night an American sentry would shoot me. Often in the pillbox my buddies and I plotted together. We were old men equipped with Panzerfausts we never learned to fire. Our feet ached. But there was one in the corner who might snitch. What could we do?" How strained were watchful eyes and ears before they revealed themselves to each other in the intimacy of the pillbox! "You are a traitor to the Kingdom? Me too! Me too!"

"But you must admit," said the little Michel, "Hitler did a lot of fine things for Germany. The National Socialist idea was a good one. In practice, they made mistakes. I was not always in agreement with them."

"Well, exactly what did you not agree with? The way they lost the war?"

"Yes. They should never have lost the war. Too much graft. Too much for the Party."

"You will have it again," warned the Bavarian, a judge advocate general in the Munich Service Corps, "The Prussians just love militarism. They love to drill. Back in 1936 I came upon a company in the woods practicing falling on their bellies and getting up with precision. My brother laughed at them. I cried. I said, 'They love it. They always have.' The Prussian pig, he just likes war and nothing can knock it out of his head. I always hated them. I am a Bavarian, not a Prussian pig, but what could I do?"

The little old man in Garmisch looked nutty but he had been keeping his lists, meticulous lists for the day of reckoning. He was the scorned clerk in the Rathaus who had once repeated some joke about Mussolini being a buffoon. He would have been dismissed if not for the intervention of his wife's brother, who was a big shot in the Labor Front and did not want political prisoners in his family, as well as a load of hungry mouths to feed. They thought the clerk was simple, but he twitched and squirmed and kept his eyes and ears open. The records might disappear but he knew who was a Nazi, who was a fiery Nazi, a fanatical Nazi, a Nazi by compulsion, a Nazi ruffian, a hidden Nazi. Every day his lists swelled with more and more Nazis. Nazi class of 1924, Nazi class of 1933, Nazi class of 1940, Nazi class of 1942. That one was of the Gestapo and that one of the ss. He noted every little slight and petty act of persecution. And soon his lists named half the town.

Garmisch was at the foot of the Bavarian Alps and the place swarmed with the plump wives of officials who had sent their households out of the danger zone of the big cities for the protection of their descendants and for their own pleasure. There was always a Blitz Mädel in a Munich terror bombing; in their distraction did they know what they were doing? They would visit their wives on weekends when it was convenient, consuming the last cans of gas for which the Wehrmacht's tanks were panting. And when Nuremberg and Munich fell they stayed on in little Garmisch. They bought themselves short leather pants and suspenders decorated with the edelweiss and they were jolly fat Bavarians like the rest of them. But they had not counted on the avenging arm of the little clerk, who ferreted them out.

"Come, I'll show you a barn where there is a general. A real general."

"Well, Herr General, what are you doing in this mal-odorous spot? A general in a haystack."

"I was sent here for my health. My lungs, you know."

I denounce you. You denounce me. We denounce him. I want your house. You want my job. Whose bread I eat, his song I sing. Curry my favor now or else. Who has the ear of the American authorities? Who can get you a travel pass? Who can get you wood? Me, the despised one. "Gods! Get him out of my hair before we have the whole town locked up."

There were thousands who remained loyal to their Führer even after his death and they wept over his fate. Many little Michels kept their feelings secret, but bits of nostalgia surfaced, to join the cacophony of the disenchanted. "When the Führer was at the helm, those who were unemployed got work, those who were hungry were fed, those who were without a roof were housed, those who were pregnant got mother's care, those who were desirous got pregnant. It made the other peoples of the world jealous and they conspired against him. He helped the poor German man, gave him dignity, and the junkers were envious of the strong new German to whom the Führer had opened up the road. And they sold him. On July the twentieth they made an attempt on his life. Well do we remember. And when that failed through a miracle such as had not before happened in world history, they sold him to the English. They lied to him, kept the truth from him, delivered him to the Americans for gold and left us to starve. The generals have their gold and we hunger. When the Americans came they tore his picture from our public places and from our homes. But never can they tear his image from our hearts. They will say he was insane. They will berate him and a thousand tongues of his betrayers will join them. But we know he was a good man and worked for us. How he labored day and night that we might live in peace, surrounded though we were by great empires bent on our destruction, the capitalists and the Jews and the Bolsheviks.

"Generals who led his armies broke their sacred oaths. We never have. In the secret recesses of our hearts are memories of the music, the cakes, and the butter. He would have given each of us a Volkswagen if he had been able. The great highways were already built. And what festivals! How we wept with joy! Will we forget the transports of delight that carried us with him to the heavens when he spoke to us? What child whose head he patted will forget him? Other men had their pleasures of wife and children. He was alone. As he said to his detractors, 'Germany is my bride.'"

To the very end the Germans had hoped for salvation — a break between Russia and the other Allies. A political victory to right the balance of the military defeat. As the prospects grew dimmer they put out tentacles in both directions. At any moment they were willing to join the Western Allies against Russia or the Russians against the Western Allies. There was always a Russian party and a Western party in Hitler's entourage. The old German whore was offering herself to the highest bidder again, to any bidder. "I, Germania, am in the heart of Europe. If you will have me, Russia, I join with you against them. If they will have me, I join with them against you." It was inconceivable that nobody should want Germania.

In May 1945 there were no buyers. We had remembered. By the fall the buyers reappeared — on the political black market of course, not yet in open courtship. There was only a tickle, but the old strumpet was refurbishing herself and assuming her mincing ways. You think that you are immune to her charms and her disease because of the good sense of the dirt farmers of Kansas and Missouri. But she had you before, when the corn was just as green.

# 5

## LOVE, HUNGER, AND WEREWOLVES

N THE THIRTY YEARS' WAR, the peasants of Germany watched their farms burn to the ground and saw their wives raped by marauder bands who fought in the service of Wallenstein or Tilly, Gustavus Adolphus or the Emperor. Catholics and Protestants disemboweled each other for their mutual salvation. Barons taxed and robbed their groaning peasants in order to participate in the military parade, loyal to one princelet today and another tomorrow, depending upon a religious crisis or a vision on the heath or a quarrel at the hunt.

The peasants became surfeited with the *soldatesca* and they rebelled. In secret they gathered with their neighbors and swore mighty oaths of union for mutual protection. Yokels by day, by night they struck down isolated mercenaries, retrieved horses that had been levied, drove stolen cattle back to their barns. At midnight courts in caves and in clearings in the brush the peasants condemned the drunken soldiers of fortune to hang. In the daylight soldiers were unable to identify an avenging peasant beneath the mask of the subservient lout. Were they men that waylaid bands of armed warriors in the fog and left their mark, or were they hungry wolves? Or were they of the Werewolf, half-man and half-wolf?

In the early months of 1945, Himmler, Kaltenbrunner, and Skorzeny, in imitation of Germanic folkways dear to the people, adapted the werewolf for current military operations behind enemy lines. The most reliable ss units and the toughest mountain divisions were subjected to an intensive recruiting campaign. "Do you want to join the Werewolf, Hans? You get out of the army, receive extra rations. Just bide your time and wait for orders. Anybody who joins will become a member of a cell of four males, trained for secret missions, in addition to which there will be one Werewolverine to do the cooking. Plenty of food has been hidden away in mountain chalets and in caves. Arms well calcimined have been dropped to the bottom of ponds and planted deep in holes in the earth."

As the first mounds of sacred German soil were occupied by the enemy, a chorus of werewolves echoed through the land. The Werewolf will get you, Yankees. Lily the Werewolf, sister of Lily Marlene, seduces you in the night. Who is she? *Wer? Wer? Wer?* (Who? Who? Who?) She will strike down the isolated soldier in his jeep, the MP on patrol, the fool who goes a-courting after dark, the Yankee braggart who takes a backroad.

When night falls on Old Rothenburg, the moon shines over the walls, and the medieval pitched-roof houses in the narrow, crooked, blacked-out streets cast weird shapes on one another. Yankee lover, what is that behind you? The outline of a man or of a wolf? Don't turn now. The window shutter in the attic across the way creaks. Ping! Am I dead? Shot in the back in the shadow of the cathedral? Or is it just a GI discharging his weapon in drunken sport? Why do they fill the niches with these grotesque statues?

"Come on, Heinrich Gartner, speak up, we've got the goods on you. We know you're SD (Sicherheitsdienst, German Security Service). Where are the headquarters of the Werewolf? From whom do you get your orders?"

"Nobody knows. The basic organization is the same as in all secret societies. Nobody in a lower echelon in the Order of Werewolves knows anything about anybody in a higher echelon. Each cell receives its orders and obeys. You know only the members of your own cell, so that if you are caught and interrogated the damage is minimal. At the moment we are trying to enroll people who have not been identified with Party and Gestapo activities, people like the little tailor and the meek-looking shoemaker. I had been commanded to recruit werewolves in every town in the northeastern section of the Gau. But I really have not had much luck with my prospects, except among a few seventeen-year-olds and they are not the best material."

"What do you think, Heinrich Gartner, now that you are a confessed member of the German Security Service? Speaking frankly, do you think we shall have much trouble with the Werewolf?"

"Well, speaking frankly as you ask me to, I think it all depends on how you treat the little Michels. If you feed them enough and treat them well the Werewolf will not get very far. If you starve them it will be more difficult. Then despair will drive them into our ranks."

"Blackmail! That's what it is. Still playing the old game of wanting appeasement. Well, there will be no Werewolf in my bailiwick. Bürgermeister, this Werewolf problem is getting rather troublesome. We hold you personally responsible. I hear from higher headquarters that the werewolves are still being recruited in this area. How can we get hold of them?"

"What about a poster?" timidly suggested Bürgermeister Dr. Peters. And in due time the posters, bold black on yellow, were plastered on the walls: "All members of the local Werewolf organization and all members of nonlocal Werewolf organizations who, in pursuit of their functions or otherwise, shall find themselves within the confines of Lamprechtheim at the time of the publication of this order, shall report to Room 8 on the Third Floor of the Rathaus without fail on or before 20 May 1945. Violation of this directive will be punishable in accordance with Order No. 87 of the Allied Military Government."

"That ought to get them!"

But the sign of the Werewolf kept reappearing on white walls — a vertical line, traversed in the middle by a horizontal line that at one end had a vertical line perpendicular to it, pointing upward. Most members of the Counterintelligence Corps were of the opinion that it was merely a hastily drawn swastika. Others described it as a runic symbol. One folklorist maintained that it represented an iron prong thrust into a tree and baited with meat to ensnare wolves. The wolf would jump for the meat, catch his snout on the prong, and hang there. This ingenious reading of their logo had hardly any relevance to the activities of the Werewolf. Nor had Hitler's summons of April 1 succeeded in persuading loyal Germans to join them.

When Allied telephone wires were cut, the most thorough investigations usually revealed nothing more than the growing practice among German women of snipping pieces from the maze of telephone wire for clotheslines. "In the end we shall of course demoralize you as the Maquis demoralized us," predicted Heinrich Gartner in a confidential mood. "In my library in Stuttgart I have one of the best collections in the world of writings and reports on the organization of clandestine groups from the beginning of time. There are very few tricks the modern underground has adopted that were not in the standard equipment of the Carbonari. Perhaps modern operatives have more electrical and chemical devices at their disposal, but that does not heighten the element of surprise. It is just like modern magicians and their elaborate gadgets as contrasted with the genius of a Cagliostro. Men come to rely too much on their tools, to the neglect of their ingenuity. The modern underground in Europe has yielded nothing novel. During our invasion Belgians and Frenchmen hid weapons in coffins and under the skirts of nuns just as they did in the last war. At the moment we do not believe in the feasibility of successful performance. Any premature outbreak on our part would only result in a negative reaction among the ordinary people. But later, later, it may be a different story."

In the little towns, such ominous words were drowned out by the complaining — or cajoling — voices of the German Michels. "The Russians are coming! The Russians are coming! Why are the Americans abandoning us to the Russians? It is not right what they are doing. What will become of us when the moujiks arrive?"

"Oh, it won't be so bad. Remember what they said the Americans would do; well, it was exaggerated. Maybe the Russians are really not so horrible. Did you hear what the ration is in Berlin as announced over the radio? If they give us more to eat, we will have to like them better."

"Wish you could stay, Yankee soldier. You're so sweet and you've got a sack full. And you're so clean. Moujiks are dirty. You look like Hans. And you have chocolate and cigarettes and soap. Maybe tomorrow you'll bring me a teensy-weensy piece of soap. You smell so good. Of all the foreign nations we love you best. What fine trucks you have! What white bread you eat! It is just like cake for Easter. Why don't they let you talk to us? It's mean of General Eisenhower to be so harsh. We are only poor women. You be good to us and there will be no trouble."

Yankee soldier stands guarding a lonely bridge through the night on the autobahn linking Weimar and Jena and Erfurt. *"Ik dik lieb. Schlafen. Schlafen.* You're dangerous stuff, baby. Well, for Christ's sake, it's worth it. What the hell can I do with the damn cabbage? So you get caught. I've been in worse scrapes before."

Roll me over, Yankee soldier,
Roll me over, lay me down,
And do it again.

"I was just asking her for the direction, sir."

"Let's wrestle. Your flowers are pretty. *Compris?* I mean *verstehen?* I give you *kaw-gumi,* you give me *schnapps.* Gee, this is some road along here, just like the Lincoln Highway. And clean. Boy, these people are clean compared to those dirty frogs. And remember Italy. It makes me itch just to think of it. These kids are hot stuff."

The u.s. Psychological Warfare Board became worried about the disproportionate number of German females to males. "The women are repressed and when people are repressed they might do almost anything. It is bad for their morale and for public order. They will become neurotic and again be a danger to the peace of Europe. You just cannot suppress normal instincts; it is plainly impossible. Why, they're doing it in every cellar and under every tree."

"These girls don't tease. They know what you want right off. They understand a guy. A bunch of castrated old majors in headquarters may make the rules and then break them in secret. The GI gets screwed."

"You mean he doesn't."

Down by the river they were bathing. Not naked but they might as well have been. And they disported themselves in the sun. "What flanks! Built like a brick shithouse. What a chassis! Nutty brown. And blond hair."

Yankee soldiers sat with field glasses and stared at their prisoners of two days ago in dalliance with the firm female flesh. "What a war! Who won it anyhow?"

"Well, we're showing them. Be dignified. Preserve what you got. Beware of the venereal rate."

"She's not a German, sir. She told me she was Russian."

"Well, how come you asked her in the first place?"

"We're beginning to look ridiculous in their eyes. You cannot make eunuchs out of a bunch of red-blooded American boys."

"You don't have to move out, honey chile. Just stay around the place and cook for us."

"I hear they're relaxing the order. We can fraternize with children. Well, what is a child? I like mine about sixteen years old."

"When the boys leave, I'd like to see them go in silence. We did our job. Mission accomplished, then depart. Let them remember us as strong, silent Americans. After the way they massacred our boys in the Ardennes, after these concentration camps and crematoriums, how can you kiss one of them!"

And when it's all over, what will you remember? What will inhabit your dreams, Yankee soldier? That sizzling blond in Heilbronn. The 88s that killed your buddies will be forgotten. Your rage at the first sight of Dachau, the years of your life you gave to beat these bastards will be blotted out.

"Good-bye darling. I'll be back soon."

Hunger! Hunger! The word is the same in English and German. He points to his belly and opens his toothless mouth and mumbles, "Hunger, hunger" to make you understand. They gape at American soldiers carrying their weekly rations of cigarettes, soap, and candy as if they were walking show-cases. The kids jump on the jeeps and stare. *Nix Schokolade. Nix Schokolade. Kaw-gumi. Kaw-gumi.* You cannot hate kids. No American can. The persistence and utter helplessness of little kids. "Gee, these flaxen-haired kids look like my own. They make my heart sort of jump every time I see them."

Unlike the country towns, in the cities the food was not too plentiful. You cannot live well on 1,800 grams of bread a week, with a drop of butter and a square inch of meat a month. Try sleeping with a girl regular and not feeding her, coming in full bellied when she hasn't had enough grub. You just can't do it. And you begin to filch a bit of food here and there for her. The boys who are closest to the mess are the luckiest. Then begin the fights between those caught filching and those who have no desire, between those Germans who have a Yankee lover in their midst and those who do not, for there are not enough Yankee soldiers to go around and an in-determinate proportion are total abstainers. Love and food. Sex and hunger. Occupation is primitive business.

6

## REVOLT OF THE SLAVES

A LATVIAN WAS BUYING BREAD in the marketplace in Bad Tölz when suddenly a bunch of ex-Dachau inmates jumped on him. They recognized him as one of their guards. "We get to know our guards. I swear by my dead wife and children. I'll bring you twenty others who'll identify him. He is ss."

"Jesus Christus Maria! Me! I'm not ss."

"Inmates never make a mistake. Through the years the faces and movements of every guard have become part of us. We studied them, waiting for the day. Their lousy mugs were engraved upon our memories and upon our bodies with the sticks they used to torture us. We remember. They beat their faces into us."

"Jesus Christus Maria! I am an Ostarbeiter (laborer from the East) from Riga. They made a mistake."

"For years I waited for this day. I'm a political prisoner and a Social Democrat. My partner with whom I was engaged in smuggling tobacco wanted the whole of the business for himself. I did not know that he had secretly been a Party man for years. He turned me over to the Gestapo, and for ten years they kept me in concentration camps. Ten years. Now I swear by all that is dear to you and me that he is ss. If the beasts are allowed to run around free you will have trouble with them."

"Jesus Christus Maria, I'm innocent! They brought me here with the other Ostarbeiter. Me ss! O my poor sister!"

"Just leave him to us inmates. We'll tear him to pieces."

"O Jesus Christus Maria, I'm not ss! I strip for you. Strip to the waist. Nothing tattooed on my arm. I'm a Latvian Ostarbeiter who worked in a machine shop."

"Bang your head against the wall if you want. Mind you, against the wall, not against that elegant Bavarian tile stove. This Dachau man with the shaven head says you *are* ss."

When the Hun disgorged his Russian slaves they gave the German burghers of Neustadt-an-der-Weinstrasse the scare of the war. "You bandit! You Fascist! I kick you in the arse, you bandit, you Fascist! You wanted everything. Work, work, work for you. You go fuck your mother now. Now *you* work."

"Help! Help! They are killing him. American, American, have pity. Ivan is drunk. He is beating him to death. You promised to protect us from these beasts. Look! Look! Is that the way you preserve order in the face of these wild animals?"

"Fascist bandit! Persecutor of the working classes! Bourgeois! Capitalist! Take this and this and this!"

"Herr Captain! Your duty! Stop him! Stop him!"

"Madam, you do not understand. That is a political dispute they are having. We are democrats and believe in freedom of discussion. There is a political difference of opinion between them. One says the other is a Fascist. Being a Russian, he is presumably a Communist. We do not interfere in politics. I am a soldier. He won't kill him, I trust."

"The bandits! The Fascists! The counterrevolutionary bourgeois murderers!"

In the heyday of victory the Germans had conducted raids in Warsaw and scooped up Poles who were not Jews. They drove everything that walked on two feet out of Dvinsk. They ordered Pétain who ordered Laval who ordered Darnand who kidnapped the seventeen-year-olds in the villages of Lorraine and the idle ones coming out of the movies in Paris. They seized the Italian navy in Greece and anyone in Hungary, Romania, and Yugoslavia who could groom a horse. Eighty-year-olds and unborn babes were destined to see the sun rise in the Third Reich. Girl children became women soon enough and boys became predatory animals. The subjugated peoples of Europe were shipped in freight cars and unloaded all over the Reich. To each one they handed a yellow card identifying the bearer as a worker of the Reich, along with an admonition to treasure the card as an amulet. With it you had status, without it you were dead.

And then the cards got jumbled. Nobody knew how many cards were issued, not even Sauckel the slave master. Some say that at one time there were seven million of them, men, women, and children. In the offices of the General Plenipotentiary for Manpower the slave laborers were mixed up with the political prisoners of occupied countries, the Allied prisoners of war, the nationals of the Axis partner who had withdrawn prematurely, and the voluntary laborers imported from the satellite Balkans.

Now that Germany was being crushed in the vise of foreign armies, what should the masters do with their slaves? They were valuable man-woman-child hours of labor. As long as they had slaves for the underground factories all was not lost. They herded them north and south and east and west in a frantic attempt to keep them behind the battle lines. Those who survived the bombings of the factories were dispersed upon the land and allocated among the peasants, who measured out victuals to the two-footed ones. How much fodder can keep this creature alive and pulling? Is he really worth his sustenance? Better a good horse. But the Wehrmacht requisitioned the horses for their transport, leaving Russians and Poles in their stead. During the day they worked in the fields. At night they were squeezed into barracks. Supervisory manpower was scarce, and the smallest possible space allotted to each slave made guarding them that much easier.

Back in the spring of 1942, Dr. Johannes von Detrius estimated that he needed 564,000 man-woman-child hours of labor for the crops in Swabia. He figured that the laborers would consume a maximum of 183,642 man-woman-child hours of food, computed in accordance with the standards for foreign laborers established by the Health Institute, which left a net addition of 380,358 man-woman-child hours of labor for the Reich (not taking into consideration the transport costs, which were, after all, not his problem but belonged in the department of Dr. Bernhard). So they grabbed them up from Poltava in the Ukraine and brought them to Neustadt-an-der-Weinstrasse and distributed them in accordance with the tabs and the files in the Department for the Supervision of Foreign Workers. At first they starved them. But as the boundaries of the Reich shrank and the sources of supply diminished, the slaves became a more valuable commodity and the Propaganda Ministry began to publish articles in the illustrated supplements of Max Amann's newspaper chain about how happy the foreign workers were.

Then came the Americans. Russians and Serbs and Frenchmen broke out of typhus-ridden barracks. The doctors of all nations tried to keep them in their cages, but how could the doctors confine them after their appointed hours? The typhus germs spread over the countryside.

A sort of pidgin German was the international language of the slaves. "We are from Poltava. Me and him and her. We are all from Poltava. The whole village — men, women, and children — were brought here to work. They kept us in the Sedan Kaserne on the edge of town. Heaped into rooms like cattle, only without straw. Men, women, and children."

"Who is he?"

"He's my Kavalier, a good Kavalier. He brought me to eat."

"Where did he get it?"

"I don't know. The men go to work *schanzen*. All day long digging ditches. Then they steal off to a cellar and find onions and jelly and he brings me. A good Kavalier. Sometimes they get caught. That is not good. Then they beat them on the buttocks with iron sticks while everybody watched. His buttocks were swollen like a woman in the ninth month and I had nothing to rub them with. He is a good Kavalier. He promised to marry me.

"Your bombers thought there were German soldiers here and so they hit the Kaserne. Maybe it was because of the

Kaserne down the hill. We were afraid and we prayed. You hit only one side, but you killed a lot of horses. That day they took the men out to work and when the guards were not looking the men cut big chunks off the dead horses. The horsemeat tasted bad but it was good. Katya ate it without cooking but I wouldn't. At night we sang and we cried and the guards rushed in and turned everything we cooked in upside down."

"Protect us from these drunken Russians, Americans. Up on the hill they murdered a farmer by beating him over the head with clubs. His brains spilled out on the floor."

"A doctor! A doctor! Come in, Herr Dr. Franzl. This woman is ill."

"No, for the love of God, not him. In the name of the Committee of Workers from the Poltava area I demand that he immediately be sent away. He is not a doctor. He is a butcher of the working classes. Whenever anyone came and said he was sick, he sent him to work even with coughing and fever. I demand that we immediately be returned to the Soviet Union."

"That one's a troublemaker, that's what he is. Man, there's a war on. There are transportation problems. You think American trucks grow on trees?"

"To the motherland! Which road leads direct from Neustadt to Poltava? First, food for the journey. Sack the warehouses and smash the store windows!"

Terror gripped the vintners of Neustadt-an-der-Weinstrasse, for the slaves were on the loose. "Anna, hide the hens, bury the eggs. Dig deep. And let's lock ourselves in. The Russians are coming. Stop! Help! They are stealing and burning."

There were barrels and barrels of wine, and the slaves celebrated a Kermess. "O the lovely Don, the flowing Don! Play the guitar, Ivan, and let's dance a Kazatski. Mussolini *kaput.* Soon Hitler *kaput. Alles kaput. Alles kaput.*"

"See here, Russians and Poles, drink like gentlemen. We know you've had a hard time of it, but no use abusing the privileges." If only they would not tear open the sacks of flour, but they are wild. They cook soup and then they vomit. They drink anything at a gulp. Wood alcohol paralyzes and kills them. We restrain them only for their own good.

"Help! Help! A Russian with a knife threatened to kill me if I did not sell him bread. But you know I can't sell him bread without ration coupons. He chased my husband around the bakery."

"*Chleb, chleb* for the victorious Allies. The food you soldiers give us is good — we are not complaining — but it is too fat to eat without bread. We are not used to it."

"But the baker cannot in accordance with the existing regulations bake more than a certain number of loaves a day and he has already gone beyond his quota."

"I didn't have any salami and he had salami. Everybody had salami but me. He stole out of the kitchen. His room is stinking with food from the boxcars down by the railroad station. I am dissatisfied. In the name of the Soviet government I lodge a protest. For three years we sweated here without a mouthful to eat except filthy soup. And now that we've been liberated we want to be free to go."

"But you do not understand. You are free. Just register your name and exchange your German card for an American card."

"Help! Help! He is breaking into my house. I am all alone. My husband is on the eastern front. Have pity!"

The blond-haired moujik reeled in a stupor, speechless. What should I do to him? Lock him up as *they* locked him up? What does he care? *Alles egal. Alles egal.* Nothing matters.

"Russky?"

"No, Ukrainija."

"Polsky!"

"Italiano!"

"Are you happy now? Why don't you show it? What makes you all look so glum? Glum, that's it. You've got liquor and women and food. Why are you so brutish instead of behaving like free men? You, Babutchka, with the face of a shriveled apple and a pug nose, why can't you smile?"

"What is there to smile about? *Rabotya, rabotya. Immer rabotya.* Work, work. Always work. I don't want to go home. Poltava is all burned down. Here I have a barn to sleep in. At home it's cold."

"Not so in Napoli. When do we go back to Italia, Signor? *O bella Italia.*"

"Armando, Giuseppe, how did you get along?"

"They liked us for what we had. We liked them too for what they gave us. Fair exchange. Once for a cigarette, twice for bread. How can one rape a German woman? They all want it. Armando sings for them and they give him everything. Now come you Americans and it's finished. They want *you* and we get no cigarettes."

"Mussolini kaput. His end was too quick. They should have pulled out nail by nail, hair by hair, piece by piece."

"Now back to Italia! You come with me to Italia. I'll find you a virgin of fifteen years. Italian women are much better than these Germans. And what is nicer than a virgin fifteen years old, fresh, with a soft, luscious body?"

"Do you know what? Taking a crap is better. The Pope tried it out once. He asked a monk who had not taken a crap or had a virgin for a long time what he wanted most and the monk took a crap."

"It was not so bad here. I got along. But *Italia, bella Italia.* I'm happy now."

The French held themselves aloof from the other slaves. They were among the oldest foreign inmates of the Reich and had learned the ropes. They knew their worth as a labor force and were Western European rationalists. No mixing them up with eastern peasants or Italians, who were dominated by the requirements of animals, who didn't know how to milk cows badly or plow inadequately. The fellow who got along in the dives of Montmartre and Marseilles could twist one of these German thickheads without the fool even noticing it. *On se débrouille.* Food and a bed and a woman and *je m'en fous.* He replaced the drafted German in the field and in the bedchamber. The gamin of Paris who became a farm laborer did not overwork. French proletarians knew the technique of the slowdown and the acts of sabotage that could not be detected or pinned onto anybody in particular. In the camps, literary Frenchmen devised little games to keep madness from their souls. They held competitions, and prizes were awarded by a formal decision of a jury after the manner of the Prix Goncourt. They had French culture to preserve. And the Germans did not completely disdain them. Forced laborers who were kidnapped at random in cities and towns of conquered France probably did the Reich as much harm as good. These were old enemies, the Frenchman and the Boche. They had sized each other up.

The Poles became the bearers of the anti-Russian rumor. DP camps were hotbeds of tales of the impending conflict between the Russians and the Americans. Poles would not return to Poland. They would wander the earth like the Jews and the Irish. Poles, the most partitioned people in Europe. London Poles and Lublin Poles. "Please, Panye, don't send me back to the Russians, they will kill me. I don't want to go with them. I don't want to stay with the Germans either. We yearn for another Poland. We were the first victims and we shall be the last to be saved." Elegant Polish officers of the London Repatriation Service flew in to represent the languishing London Polish Government. Nobody quite knew where anybody wanted to be repatriated.

"The DPs hate one another as much as they hate the Germans. You can't put a Russian and a Pole in the same room without their knifing each other. Give them some liquor and they're ready to tear the place apart."

I devised a scheme to preserve a semblance of order by tranquilizing the Russian contingent in the camp. Having discovered a Jew from Poltava named Ashkenazi, who had passed for a Volga German, I gave him a badge and delivered a solemn declaration: "You are hereby appointed representative-in-chief of the Russians kidnapped as slave labor from Poltava and Odessa and points east, herded into Neustadt and Tauberbischofsheim and points west. This armband with the MG sewn upon it is the symbol of your authority. It is bestowed upon you in the name of General Eisenhower. Henceforth it is your duty to keep your countrymen in good and civil order. They shall remain within the confines of this school building. Self-restraint and orderliness." Then I turned to the rest: "Behave in a manner worthy of the great Marshal Stalin. Contrary to what you may have heard, you no longer have to work for the Germans. You are liberated, and as soon as your government through official plenipotentiaries arranges for your repatriation, you will leave for your native land. In the meantime, keep the place clean."

Finally the trucks came and hauled the slave laborers and their piled-up junk back to their homelands. French to the west; Russians to the east; Italians to the south; Poles nowhere.

# 7

## REMNANTS OF ISRAEL

**T**HEY WERE LOCKED INTO BOXCARS, the remnants of Israel, the very old and the very young. Living in the pale, the isthmus of Europe between the Black Sea and the Baltic, they had been mowed over three or four times by the Germans and yet not all had been annihilated. Even the most efficient reapers miss a few. There is always a remainder for the gleaners.

They had been shifted from camp to camp, put to work when labor demand conquered ideology, burned when they were in excess. They hid in the sewers of Augsburg, in monasteries where the abbot was protective, in the beer halls of the Gestapo, in the most obvious and the most unlikely places. When the days of their persecutors were numbered, they were herded into cattle cars, shoved into wagons, driven up and down the kingdom in compliance with contradictory orders.

But Eisenhower in his headquarters was master of the skies and had decreed that nothing was to move in Germany until he arrived. The trains were to stop in their tracks. Anything that traveled by day or by night would imprint itself upon a photoplate and be bombed to blazes.

The train slowly mounting the hill, heavy-laden with the sorrows of Israel, was smacked right in the middle, then machine-gunned. The occupants jumped or were thrown out of the boxcars and fled into the woods for cover. "Why must salvation be a Jabo (the popular German name for the American fighter plane)? We are Yidalach, little Jews. Enough, enough. We can bear no more." And they lay in the forest, dying.

Among them was one who never wailed, a doctor from Lodz. His blood had turned to ice and his heart to stone. He walked to a nearby town held by the Americans and sought out an officer. Together they drove to the hospital at Sankt Otilien, where they broke in on recuperating ss troopers engaged in a spring bacchanalia with their devoted nurses. The Americans emptied the wards of the amorous German wounded who were ambulatory and quartered them in the town. Squads of inhabitants were ordered to gather the dying Jews who had taken refuge in the forest. The Germans searched the woods as commanded, but the Jews, bewildered and frightened at the sight of their enemies, were reluctant to come out. The American officer calmed them. They helped each other into baby carriages and carts without horses. Those who could shuffle along pushed their brothers who were nearer death. Back in the hospital of Sankt Otilien two and three were packed in a bed. The doctor of Lodz ministered to them in grim silence.

The next day an old rabbi from Berdichev asked permission to conduct a funeral. The American officer corralled the ss to dig a mass grave, for by then twenty or thirty Jews a day were dying. And a guard of German officers was forced to stand by and help lower the bodies into the common pit.

KOADDISH FOR BURIAL OF THE DEAD

Magnified and sanctified be His great name in the world which He hath created according to His will. May He establish His kingdom during your life and during your days, and during the life of all the house of Israel, even speedily and at a near time, and say ye, Amen.

When the rabbi had performed the ritual he raised his voice to the heavens and cried aloud his lamentation. "O God, we bury our brethren in accordance with your law. They did not live to see the day of their salvation. Like Moses, they could gaze upon the promised land in the distance, but they could not enter it. That was your will.

"When a Jew is found dead, it is customary for those who bury him to repeat, 'We have not shed this blood. The shedding of this blood is not on our heads.' Can we say this now? Who is to blame? Is Haman the wicked one who set out to destroy us all, man, woman, and child, to blame? Who knows? Are these men standing here to blame? How did these victims die and for what purpose? We all must be blamed. We all are at fault. We all are full of sin.

"Oh when will an end come to our suffering? For thousands of years we have been shunted from pillar to post. Why? What have we done, we little people? What do we want but to live out our years?

"Whom are we burying here? Who knows them? There are some whose names we never learned. Whose son and whose father are they? These are our sons and our fathers and our sisters and our brothers.

"Let not the Germans who are standing here feel that we are full of hate. Because we are not. We leave judgment to God. The crimes are too grave for man to understand, to believe that they come from man. What good is vengeance to these nameless ones?"

Bodies of Jews are rotting in the rose bowers everywhere in Germania and they should never be forgotten. Retain the image of their corpses in your mind's eye, for in this beautiful land nothing is visible above ground but the rolling hills, every acre neatly tilled in shades of green and yellow, with the purple haze of the mountains in the distance and a well-preserved castle here and there.

In the short time at the disposal of the Boche, despite his many preoccupations incident to the conduct of a war on two fronts and the clearing of rubble after the bombings, he managed to have six million Jews who were not at war killed, and to reignite in the hearts of the countries of Europe a loathing for the Jews, who were being turned to soap to wash away his bloodstains. There was system in hunger and in torture and in death.

Remember the massacres of the Middle Ages, the Rhineland — Speyer, Worms, and Mainz — a vale of tears to the Jewish communities. Read the simple chronicle of Rabbi Ephraim of Bonn, who recorded by name and place of birth each Jew and his wife and children and told how they were slaughtered by the Crusaders of an earlier Reich. Seven centuries later in Belsen there was not even a scribe to commemorate the dead; just orderly bookkeeping of the victims by number. The gas chamber had its stated capacity, like the steel mill.

According to the Book of Esther, Haman the wicked one was hanged from a gibbet many cubits high for publishing letters throughout the lands of the Persians and the Medes calling upon the peoples of the empire to slaughter the Jews on the fourteenth day of Adar. Mordecai, cousin of the beautiful Queen Esther and leader of the Jews, was presented with a new cloak that same day and he became the chief adviser to King Ahasuerus. But this time vengeance was *verboten*. Mordecai remains behind barbed wire in Belsen pending further negotiations, until proper arrangements can be made for his disposition. As for the followers of Haman, they are busy writing their memoirs. The traditions of Anglo-Saxon common law amalgamated with the principles of Roman law as embodied in the Napoleonic Code require due process and trial by tribunals without passion, hate, wrath, vindictiveness, or other low elements of the soul.

"How can *we* help you, little Jew? Don't bother us."

"My noble sir, we have a small community of 85 in Leipzig, remnants of Israel — some had married Aryan women and were allowed to stay on for a few years, others have returned from Dachau, Auschwitz, and Buchenwald; there are Mischlinge (halfbreeds), and those who survived in secret. One of our number died and we needed a piece of black cloth for the burial ceremony. I went from one German ration officer to another and they said that coupons were required and there was no provision for us under the law. Now, is that right?"

"It was not proper what they did to the Jews," acknowledged the German Michel, "it could all have been arranged differently. It was not necessary to burn the synagogues. Of course, we knew nothing about it." Thousands of German Jews disappeared from under foot, from some of the best apartments and most luxurious villas, and a substantial number of purchasers were found to offer quick prices; but they, the mass of the Germans, of course knew nothing about it.

"Well, let bygones be bygones. We have all suffered enough. Let us turn over a new leaf."

"But the dead, the six million dead. Have they no rights?"

"The sooner we forget about them the better."

"Well, the Jewish problem remains a problem. If they would return to us perhaps the Jewish international financiers would exert their influence and we could get more calories in our rations."

"By the way, how many calories are allowed a Jewish former inmate of Buchenwald?"

"We add 825 calories as compensation for his suffering. We cannot always provide him with a dwelling unit because in the existing shortage it would complicate things and violate the housing regulations. We cannot treat the Jews very differently because that would be discrimination. Hence we act with impartiality toward all the inhabitants of the Reich."

What do you want, remnants of Israel? Do you expect them to return to you your corner department store in Frankfurt, along with your good name and your good will? Do you want your publishing house and your textile factory to be restored? And you, *doctor medicus,* who from father to son cured the Gentiles in Rothenburg, do you want to go back to the pretty town and start rolling pills for your old friends? Do you, physicists, want to write for their journals? Your ancestors forgot the massacre by the Crusaders. Will you be less forgiving?

And by the way, remnants of Israel, where else do you want to go? To *la belle France,* where *à bas les Juifs* is not a law, only a secret hiss through the Republic? To Poland, where German invaders and Poles, though they differed here and there, fed each other on the ancient hate, where killing Jews remained a pastime? There will be law in Romania, Poland, Hungary, protecting your rights, but you need more than a law. You need what they cannot give, for Europe has been poisoned.

To what other continent shall we send you? To Uganda? Tanganyika? Madagascar? The natives there don't want you any more than do the English or the Americans.

Ah, so it's the milk and honey of Palestine you're longing for, a homeland of your own, a bit of turf where you won't be an eternal alien, a resting place for the wanderer of the ages. "Well, that can't be done," said Clement Atlee, "it just can't be done. His Majesty's Government has too many relevant factors of general applicability to consider."

In Dachau there were heaps of bodies: bodies of inmates murdered by guards at the last moment before the arrival of American troops; bodies of guards who had undressed inmates and disguised themselves in their clothes but were recognized by their victims and massacred by them; bodies of guards torn limb from limb. Hungry, typhus-infected prisoners still caged were gnawing at fresh sides of beef from the ransacked butcher shops of the surrounding district. Too much raw meat of all kinds. Knee deep in flesh and blood. Enough to puke on.

The roads south of Dachau were crowded with victims let out from the concentration camps, still wearing the black-and-white striped cloth of the convict, waving, begging food when

the convoy of American vehicles stalled. Their striped gar-
ments were their pride. They had endured. Heads were
grotesquely misshapen, bashed in from beatings. They looked
like the elongated saints of El Greco — a tribe of ascetics
trudging along the highway. Where to? Eisenhower requested
them to observe military discipline and stay put until the
agents of repatriation of their respective nations appeared.
But try to control the course of a thousand rivulets after a
giant dam has burst.

See the show in Vélodrome arena in Paris, *Les Crimes
Hitlériens.* See it in pictures; it's more poignant in glossy
prints. See it at Madame Tussaud's waxworks in London,
*German Atrocities Depicted.*

"She used to be a *petite femme* who often came to the Dôme
in Paris. She looked very different then. Look what they have
done to her. O you Americans, if you only gave us as much as
you give German prisoners we would be happy. You are too
good to them, the *salauds,* the pigs." On the Boulevard Mont-
parnasse old competitors embraced the haggard women wearing the coarse cloth of the concentration camp.

"Ah, they always forget. It's just one year since I got out of
the concentration camp," reminisced an aging bar-club hostess
in Paris. "And were my friends sorry to see me! They said to
themselves: 'She has reappeared, the old hen.'"

In the typhus section of Dachau each nation of Europe had
found a flag for its group of huts and in the middle was a decorated bower of many colors with a salutation to the United
Nations. Come and see Dachau Fair, May 1945. Take a good
look at us. To you the war may be over. We are still dying here
every day. Remember us. A shriveled body becomes a fetus
again. In a decontamination center under the showers the inmates looked like embryos preserved in alcohol.

"Wandering striped men, why don't you break into the nearest house and outfit yourselves from head to foot with knickerbockers of tweed and fine wool socks? What are you afraid of?"

"It's not right. That's the way *they* did. We are not they."

"Then you are Jesus Christ. Hey, you Nazi *Hausfrau,* clothe them."

"I have no clothes to fit them. My husband was a big man. My sons were even taller. O it's horrible what they did to these poor people. Horrible. Inhuman. And for all this we must now pay."

"Who is to blame?" read the psychological warfare poster across a photogenic skeleton, pasted on a wall. "Not we," was scribbled across in answer. "Yes, we are to blame," was the retort scribbled across the answer.

The striped men dragged themselves along the gutters of the highways to keep out of the way of the Ford trucks and the plump Gretchens on their bikes. What rosy thighs you have! If only there were distributive justice on the spot so that we could give the sallow bony ones some of your pink flesh. That kind of transubstantiation would be worth believing in.

We finally got hold of him, the former commandant of the Oranienburg concentration camp, Hauptsturmbannführer of the ss, a sickly old man. Was this dilapidated creature the terror of Oranienburg? Was this the master of the whip, this smelly old man who stank with age?

"Me? What do you want with me? What do you want with an old diabetic? I have not been in Oranienburg for six years. They threw me out because I was too good to the prisoners. When I was there I received letters from Jews and political prisoners praising my administration, telling me how fair and just everything was . . ."

"How much they enjoyed their stay?"

"They had no complaints. And their wounds were healed."

"How many whippings did you witness?"

"None."

"Did you ever hear of any?"

"Yes, once or twice guards did beat prisoners but I stopped it immediately. That is why Himmler dismissed me. He said I was too soft, that I had lost my old vigor. And since then I have been living on a pittance. I never got anything out of that job. Just a lot of trouble. I am a sick man."

"You've been in the Party since 1929. Why did you join?"

"To eat. When a man is starving nothing else counts. I needed a job and I got it. What do you want of me? What good am I to you? Why don't you get Himmler? He is responsible, not me. It's all his fault."

As Wergeld for the discolored bodies, swollen thighs, broken bones, emasculated men, lacerated women, charred flesh, there was nothing but this foul old man, babbling incoherently. In his pocket was a photograph of a goose-stepping unit of the ss with this creature in its younger form passing before the reviewing stand, Nuremberg, 1934. He looked tough. He was the one who threw the first brick into the glass pane and yelled *"Jude!"* Now he stands before you, unshaven, exhaling stale breath into your face.

An eye for an eye. A tooth for a tooth. But Holy Moses, he has not got eyes enough or teeth enough for the talion law. A pound of flesh! But his diabetic rotting body has not enough flesh on it even if we settled the debt for an ounce instead of a pound. Cut his life, but he has not got years enough, this stinking old wretch. Then vengeance upon his children and his children's children unto the fourth generation. But he is barren. This toothless, childless dog comes to have justice practiced upon him. Justice wants fresh young maidens and bronzed youths worthy of her blows.

Cotton Mather could do it, but we can't. Cotton Mather and John Knox could distribute justice, but the sloppy romantics of the twentieth century lay down their arms, look up from their dead, take pride in their decorative campaign ribbons, and slobber over the vanquished and the near vanquished. Are you cold, my dear little Germans? Are you hungry? Take care of your calories or we shall have to.

In solemn assembly at Potsdam we guaranteed you individually a caloric value equal to the average of the caloric values of the surrounding countries. We take a starving Greek, a plump Dutchman, a scrawny Serb, a hollow-eyed Italian, a substantial Dane, a bony Frenchman, and we divide by whatever we divide and that's what you get. Since you are misguided heathens we are sending you a thousand professors of poetry, journalism, economics, politics, biology, and business administration to teach you the inner check, to instruct you by example that it's wrong to burn and slaughter six million Jews and make soap out of them or use their still-living bodies for the experiments of your demon scientists. We will be patient with you and you will, we hope, learn in time. For what else shall we do with you Germans, so intelligent, so workmanlike, so ingenious, with such capacity for organization?

"That is for you to decide, Herr Captain. Not for us. Once Europe was *our* problem. Now we are *yours*. You'll starve us to death. I remember the twenties. It will happen again. That's what will become of poor Germany. We shall be wiped off the face of the earth. We shall be annihilated. My poor wife and children! How we worked from early morning till late at night! What else does the German want but bread and work? Now you will swill our produce and we will go around with our tongues hanging out. It is the greatest crime in history for us to be defeated after all our toil."

"Toil for what? For the crematorium and the gas chamber?"

"Have you been to Dresden? One hundred and fifty thousand victims in one night of terror bombing. I saw the reports. You have nothing to be proud of."

"Your German newspapers said five hundred thousand. We say thirty thousand."

What is the correct figure? How appalled should one be? Thirty thousand victims worth or five hundred thousand worth? Or should one wail at the wall of history for all the war's twenty-five million dead? Or for the one little boy, age six, the only child who survived at Auschwitz? Horror does not increase in proportion with the number of victims. They only engender statistical indifference. And how is the vanquished one to make amends for this suffering of the millions which has become numerical and tabular? Is suffering competitive and shall the slogan be, "To each according to his suffering?"

How many man-hours of suffering have you endured? We will make the Germans repay you in hectares of land, tons of coal, or perhaps in kind — the spectacle of a given number of man-hours of suffering on the part of the fellow who caused it. But how can one compensate for suffering? What is the equivalent of the moment of waiting in the corridor of the Auschwitz gas chamber, or the months in a foxhole, or the years in an Aleutian Island hut?

How did the pre–Norman Saxons (not the Leipzig Saxons) ever figure out the Wergeld value of mutilated limbs when the amputated ones appeared for justice? Since there was no traffic in limbs and eyes and ears they must have established arbitrary criteria of use-value in contravention of the law of supply and demand.

As in any philosophico-juridic discussion, there are two possibilities. *Eins von den Beiden. Entweder, oder.* Either, or.

Now either the German people (in addition to the immediate circle of those involved in the processing of the bodies of the victims from life to death) knew of the massacres, or they did not.

If they knew of what was being done (which from the number of people involved in the procedures, the spread of the camps geographically, the smell of the burning flesh, the boastings of the accomplishments in newspapers, it seems impossible to deny), then they are guilty.

If they did not (which despite the hundreds of thousands of affirmations of little German Michels pleading their innocence with an abstracted look in the eye one should not believe), then they are not guilty.

If they did know, but did nothing to stop the workings of the machine that ground the flesh of the victims, thereby participating in the bloodguilt, then either they approved or they disapproved.

If they approved (and their apparent silence on this subject as well as their enjoyment as a nation and in small groups of the fruits of the victims would militate in this direction), then they are doubly guilty of knowledge and consent and the bloodguilt is on their heads.

On the other hand, if they knew and did not approve and did not make audible or visible to ears and eyes their disapproval, then they are guilty of extreme pusillanimity or the cowardice of the nonman. If they disapproved and were silent, then it was because of one of two things. Either they knew, disapproved, and were silent out of convenience, lest any protest cause their own death; or they knew, disapproved, and were silent out of a deep conviction that so great and omnipotent was the state of evil in which they lived and breathed that it was futile to raise a squeak of righteousness in Sodom.

If they were motivated by their own convenience, then they chose the death of others to their own, which is comprehensible but unpardonable. If on the other hand they were motivated by a conviction of futility, then either they were right in their objective analysis of the powers in the Reich or they were wrong.

If they were right, then either they contributed to the coming into being of this state of affairs, or they did not. If they contributed to this state of affairs, then either they made this contribution willfully and with malice aforethought or innocently and unconsciously.

The ghost of the Gaon of Vilna and the ghost of Kierkegaard went on in this manner for many days. They discovered 848 possibilities, without reckoning the combinations and the ambivalence involved in any single action, let alone combinations of actions, and in each individual instance they came to an individual conclusion.

On July first, while waiting in Paris for a boat to transfer me to the United States, I wrote the first of many letters about Jews, recalling my experiences of recent months in Germany. "In the past year I have seen so many peculiar Jewish performances. The Nazi ideology struck such deep chords in European vice that the sounds will reverberate for years after their administrative mechanism is wrecked. Here in France the openness of the old plague defies understanding. Can you imagine allowing a set of posters in subways that depict a lot of rabbinic and Semitic heads with the inscription, 'What are they waiting for?' The other night I dropped into a bistro in Montmartre, got talking with a group of middle-class Frenchmen. Since I had had a few, I was somewhat too frank in my criticism of the peculiar disease that now possesses them. The conversation became heated and when they asked me whether I was a Jew and I said of course, they said now we understand. As usual the Jews in France are the black market and the communists. Goebbels had the only German weapon that we could not get hold of."

What a diversity of uses could be made of Jews if there were need! In the last days of Leipzig before the entry of the Russian army, Polish Jews began to come around in Polish officers' uniforms. They quickly recognized the American Jewish officers and in the traditional, ingratiating manner asked, *"Ihr seit a Yid? Ich bin oich a Yid"* (Are you a Jew? I too am a Jew). And then they poured forth their tales of woe, how nobody cared for the Jews who were starving in Warsaw. They wanted to report war crimes and to narrate their experiences. For a moment they made me feel part of the victorious army of farm boys and I told them that nobody was interested in their suffering. And they said I did not have a Jewish heart. I was only trying to deny myself in them, and them in myself.

There was a doctor among them who in one disguise or another had served in a Leipzig hospital for foreigners for three years. When the Americans arrived he tried to take over the whole hospital from an ss doctor. Our military government disapproved and the Social Democratic mayor wrote him a letter firing him for incompatibility. And so he discovered me and asked for vindication. For once I tried to perform an individual act of justice and I went hither and yon and he was vindicated. After which I learned that he had engaged in all kinds of petty illegalities.

Buchenwald Jews who returned to Leipzig were forced to live in cellars because there was a shortage of rooms and the rent and housing regulations protected the existing occupants — an old Nazi wheelhorse had remained in charge of the housing setup for expediency's sake. The crazy Nazi regime kept a few Jews around in Leipzig all through the war in order to have visible symbols of the enemy.

What horror stories I could relate of Jews living for five years in the catacombs of Augsburg! Jews in the Volkssturm pretending to be Volga Germans were interrogated by me while I tried to disguise my Yiddish German. And they knew that I knew that they knew, but we kept up the comedy. This one guy had been born in Odessa; when the Germans captured the town he was a movie operator with a Russian unit. He claimed to the Germans that he was persecuted by the Russians because he had destroyed the film *Lenin in October.* Somehow he landed in a Russian labor camp in the Saar area as an interpreter. When he came across the line he had two or three sets of false papers — bombings made it easy to lose or pretend to lose one's identity. He could be a Volga German, a Russian moujik, or a Jew, depending upon the occupying power. And then he vanished into a POW pile.

I remember vividly walking through Wiesbaden with a relatively high-ranking Englishman, also a Jew, though we never discussed the point. I was strutting and he was swaggering. Ambling slowly down the middle of the road were two Jews from a camp pulling a cart behind them. With the irony that emerges when acute pain stops they looked at us and said in a flash, *"Yidalach."* We went on talking about matters of high policy involving everyone's fate, but we both knew what the skeletons in striped tatters meant.

# 8

## A HOUSEFUL OF GENERALS

IN WEILHEIM AN ANTIQUARIAN's house filled with Goethe
and Schiller and Lessing in rare bindings became a collecting
point for the defeated generals. It was a bit crowded, but the
German headquarters staffs and special liaison officers were
growing weary of running from one south German town to
another, a jump ahead of the American columns. Each night
the problem had presented itself anew: Where to next? The

quartermaster who had been dispatched to look for accommodations found the townspeople less than overjoyed at the prospect of a headquarters staff descending upon them. Too much vehicular traffic increased the risk of a raid from American planes coasting around for targets of opportunity. The generals had no stomach for a trek over the Bavarian Alps into Italy or Switzerland. What was the use? Might as well get captured in one town as the next.

German Army Group G had surrendered in the afternoon of May 6. The generals were milling about in their quarters, shaking the hand of each new arrival in a cordial manner. "Colonel General von Sachs, Lieutenant General Breitsch. When did I see you last? Your face looks familiar. Was it at Rommel's funeral? I'm sure I've met you somewhere. Were you in the East?"

"No, in Italy. The weather was better."

The trousers were pressed and the boots shone, though many of the generals had not slept for days or had just dozed over tables. There was none of that clicking of heels and no saluting. Just fellow captives waiting for chow rather impatiently. A copy of *Faust* was lying around and an artillery general thumbed through its pages as if in search of a text appropriate to the occasion. The generals were not lacking in amiability, and the drizzle was comforting because it afforded them topics of conversation about unusual weather in ordinary places. Meteorology was now a neutral subject.

"A lot of luggage, General. Where are you going, on a tour around the world?"

"I always wanted to see New York."

"Field Marshal, tut tut, don't hide your liquor in your briefcase. The next field marshal."

A general jumped up in the hallway. "Sorry, Herr Captain, the next highest in rank present is lieutenant general."

"OK, a lieutenant general will do."

In one part of the house, in the northwest corner of the library, the generals who had composed the Reich's highest court-martial sat in silence. Among them were an ex-lawyer and a one-eyed artillerist and a diminutive aviator and an ex-schoolteacher. They had condemned generals to death for not capturing towns, for failure to obey orders, for dereliction of duty. They had sat amid the documents, and with the wisdom of hindsight unraveled the actions of men in battle who had chosen left instead of right and north instead of south and today when it should have been yesterday. Their judgments ripped the diamonds from a Knight's Cross and led to the ignominy of retirement.

"Well, what do you think about Dachau? Honorable men you generals worked for."

"We knew nothing. It was forbidden to inquire into anything but that which was being inquired into. What Himmler did was veiled from us. We heard about it only vaguely. It was our understanding that the camps were sort of reform schools for political criminals. We hear about all this horror now for the first time."

"Well, what about it, judges? Responsibility! Are you responsible? Who is responsible? Who is guilty?"

"You Americans do not understand. If you comprehended the judicial, administrative, and military organization of the Reich as established by law you would know that a soldier has nothing to do with police functions, which are the functions of the police. In our official capacities on the Reich's highest court-martial we merely received charges, sifted the evidence, determined that General von Friese, for example — our last case — should have attacked from the northwest. We condemned or exonerated. Dachau is another department. No one ever visited concentration camps. Once I told Himmler what I had heard and he said that I was repeating enemy propaganda. If what you say is true they should be tried and punished."

"Who should be tried and punished? The maniacs who were culled from army hospital wards and prisons to guard the political victims and Jews? They are not very interesting, are they? Most of our headquarters staff took the trip to Dachau to see for themselves. Do you know what we said when we looked at the shriveled bodies? We did not say, 'Damn Germans.' We said, 'We despair of mankind.'"

"We knew nothing about it. We — unfortunately, perhaps — had a system that kept such unpleasantness from the people. A brother-in-law of mine who loved my sister dearly spent a summer in Buchenwald through some mix-up. Evil tongues, I imagine. We were very close, but in all the months I slept in the same huts with him at the front, he never once mentioned the place. We were as much in the dark about it as you. It would be wrong to thrust responsibility for that on the German people.

"What could we as judges do? It was our task to condemn military commanders or find extenuating circumstances. Under normal conditions we listened for weeks, even months, consulted our law books and official papers. Lately we worked under terrific strain and many handicaps. We had to peruse the papers ever faster and look at the maps ever more cursorily and often we were at a loss. Imagine a trial to determine responsibility at which key witnesses were not available because of a lack of transportation. And the number that died in the interim before judgment could be passed! To this day no one really knows whether Lieutenant General Ernst Lange should or should not have counterattacked from the south over the Oder Bridge, whether he did or did not receive the order in due form, whether he did or did not procrastinate — unless, of course, the American authorities should allow us to continue our work in the interest of military science. Many of the documents, alas, are lost forever."

A brigadier general, former parishioner of Pastor Niemöller it later turned out, was going through an emotional crisis. "I think we are to blame. All of us. Yes, we are. We must expiate our crimes. We let ourselves be betrayed by this gang. But what could we do? I was unemployed in the twenties. An engineer. And so for lack of a job I joined the army . . ."

"And became a general?"

The place was filling up fast. There were more retreating generals in the German army than we had provided for. None of them looked like the movie characters I had been accustomed to — no Erich von Stroheims, no monocles. These were businessman types.

"You see," said the air-force general to the ground-force general, "the Americans left to us the job of distributing the beds and cots. Those who came first got the beds. You, general, will have to make do with a cot, unless of course you expect one of us to take a cot and have you take a bed . . ."

"It's all the same to me. I've slept on a field cot often enough in my life."

"Well, you should have surrendered sooner and you would have gotten a bed, too," interposed the American host.

"But we did not have planes with which to fly into your laps, like our colleagues in the air force. The only time I saw a German plane in the last months was when I reached the American lines and watched those gentlemen giving up."

"By the way, gentlemen, who do you think is more to blame for the defeat, the air force or the ground force?"

"Come, come, we are all Germans here, let us not quarrel. We Germans in the heart of Europe work more per capita and think more thoughts per capita than any other people in Europe. And what have we got on our right flank and on our left flank in this battle for existence? On our left flank, looking toward the north, the French, a decadent, crapulous people whom only we could organize and compel to work. I have nothing against the French peasant, mind you. If in my declining years I were allowed to choose where I might spend the remainder of my life I would probably seek out a village in the south of France. What colors! And how polite to me the people always were during the occupation! What courtesy! Never did I have any difficulties with them. In the end, of course, their women got us. Wine and women, that explains our defeat in France. We needed Lebensraum and their population was decreasing. The Diktat of Versailles was Clemenceau's revenge. Even your own writers knew that the way Germany was deceived by Wilson was intolerable.

"But the west did not really count. It was the east that mattered. You cannot understand Russia unless you have been there. If you had only seen the misery in those hovels! That is bolshevism for you. They were about to engulf Europe and we were the outposts. We were the bulwark against the Asiatic hordes. We who were on the eastern front saw their fanaticism. The average Russian is a good fellow. Always gave us food. But the Red Army is composed of fanatics. The political commissars sent them to their death by the thousands. If you had experienced the filth and poverty of Russia you would appreciate why we took a stand against the bolshevik hordes. They are wild beasts in battle. With my own eyes I saw the mutilations that were perpetrated on our dead. All soldiers steal from the fallen, but to slice off fingers in order to filch gold rings, that is inhuman. To cut off their sexual organs — they say that was done by women commissars. No, I never saw it myself but I heard about it from a comrade in whom I have the highest confidence. We all lived in fear in Russia, for we are European just as you are — cultured, civilized. I would never allow myself to be taken prisoner on the eastern front. There was always a bullet left for that.

"We have been defending Europe against the Asiatic beasts and now come the Americans and shoot us in the back. Naturally we would rather have you. In Budapest the Russians raped every woman, from children to the very old. No one escaped. It is a fact. You could read it in any newspaper. When I think of my wife and children in Pomerania I hope they are dead. What happens to me now is a matter of indifference. I have nothing to go back to. My wife wrote me that she was prepared to take her life if the Russians came."

The generals had begun to believe their own communiqués. "Poland attacked us, murdered our brothers. Russia planned to attack us; we beat them to the punch. Why did you Americans declare war on us? What did we do to you?"

"But we didn't. You declared war on us in accordance with the Axis treaty after we declared war on the Japanese."

"Look, I'm of the vanquished, why try to make me believe that? You declared war on us, not we on you."

"No. No. It was you on us."

"Poland declared war on us, too. And England and France. But Russia was at war with us from the very beginning. And soon you will leave, go home to your skyscrapers and your Hollywood, abandoning Europe to the bolsheviks. We go under and Europe with us. The Russians are the Mongols, the

Cossacks, the Turcomans. It is better to be dead than to fall into their hands. What a fate for us who wanted only the Ukraine and the Caucasus for European development! Why should the Ukraine be Russian? Let me assure you that the Russian peasant — and I know him — was much happier with us. Our Ostarbeiter sang as they worked and were content. The Russians would have been defeated long ago if not for you. Why did you come and interfere? Russia hates civilization. They are materialists, sly, cruel, bestial. Their guerrillas attacked us behind our lines, they disrupted our communications, they burned everything before us so that we had to live in hovels infested with lice."

"Oh, I don't know about that," interrupted an elegant staff general from German Supreme Headquarters who had wandered into our line. "There were some quite nice chappies among them. Once at a party in Moscow in the old days, while on a mission, I talked with General Tukhachevsky. You could not ask for a more refined fellow. Of course, they did away with him. They are just peasant dolts, and now you Americans have given them Europe."

The German ace General Adolf Galland, with lady and jet plane, arrived to offer his services. He would demonstrate the novel jet aircraft and its potential. For weeks he had known it was over for the Wehrmacht. The skills he had honed in missions over Belgrade, Rotterdam, and London were at our disposal to salvage European civilization from destruction.

"You mean you want to fight the Japs?"

"Well, I want to fight for European civilization."

"Look here! Look here!" cried a Luftwaffe general who had had too much to drink, having succeeded in concealing his brandy despite a rather thorough frisking, "I know we are lost now, but in two weeks we will have your matériel and we will join together against the Russians. Will you see some fighting then! We will occupy the front lines. You can stay in the rear echelons. Just give us the planes and the tanks and the gas. We will spare you so many lives. I'll wager there are a lot of people in your country who would like the idea. We will never understand why you preferred the Mongol to the white European."

"Come on up to Dachau. Would you like us to arrange an excursion? Then perhaps you will be surfeited on your civilization!"

What a bore apologies can be! And what quaint people we Americans were to ask for them. We wanted the Germans to say they were ashamed of themselves. The old revival meeting is in our blood. We thought of Germany as one vast prayer-meeting tent and we expected its people to hit the sawdust, confess themselves sinners, repent, and be saved.

The morality hour was over and most of the generals had gone to bed. The ground forces of the Wehrmacht had almost five hundred generals, tired old men with a greater percentage of hypertension sufferers than any equivalent body in the world. Their ice was on the outside, and few could play the part without regular visits to the spas. These were the virtuosi in the art of land warfare as we knew it. In defeat they were fiddlers without fiddles, harpists without harps, baseball players without bats and balls. After the world series was over, these major leaguers held a continual bull session among themselves and with us on why they had lost. The stakes were pretty high and Clausewitz in his heaven was counting up the errors.

Brigadier General Brecht was an economist who had been waiting around for his formal release from the army, which on May 7 he missed by a day or two. He had not gotten along well with Speer. It had been his thankless task to compile sheets of numbers on the raw materials available for war and his numbers failed to live up to the wishes of his superiors.

"When did you begin to think the war was lost, General?"

"Why, before it began. Obviously."

Smug little man, with the right statistics. But since nobody liked his figures, he had fallen into disgrace. He read American newspapers and he drew meticulous charts, but Hitler would not look or listen — none of this American materialism for him. He had faith in the primacy of the Idea and he hired calculators to work out the mechanics. General Brecht had to play out a losing game of bridge, his favorite analogy, knowing he would go down, but by precisely how many tricks he did not presume to forecast. "You Americans bombed out our ball-bearing factories so we spread the ball bearings of Schweinfurt among little towns in the area. Eventually this dispersion as well as the original ball bearings were the ruin of Schweinfurt."

Far from being impressed by our victory, General Brecht, sardonic economist, turned the tables on us. "You had all the cards and yet you lost two, maybe three, tricks. Why did you start bombing synthetic oil plants so late in the game? If I had been in your place our transport would have been stopped long ago. And why did you target aircraft frames instead of engines? We lost because we did not hold the cards. Now you have won and the Japs may pull a dirty one on you yet. They'll give up too soon and then where will you be? That vast economic potential of yours has its responsibilities all right.

"Your bombings were disconcerting from the psycho-physiological point of view in relation to the morale of the people, but we always rebuilt after an attack. Two or three months were necessary in most instances to get a factory restarted. Just give us a few months of peace and we'll rebuild anything. After all, the past few years afforded us a bit of training in that respect." He rubbed his hands and pursed his lips. "Unfortunately, political not economic considerations were paramount in high places in Berlin. My figures show we could perhaps still have won if Hitler had not gone on playing no trump. Maybe, that is, considering the possibilities of finesse or a bluff or two. I was working on another five-year plan for new materials when you interrupted me. Now the game is yours. Go take on the Russians at the next table. Of course they hold better cards than we ever did. We sit this one out."

Most of the professional field generals of the one-hundred-thousand-man army allowed by the Treaty of Versailles were not interested in this sort of economics. Their remorse and regret were entirely in the military universe of discourse. They were at fault for not driving on England immediately after Dunkirk. "If only we had skipped that parade in Berlin and had straightaway crossed the Channel you would have had no base for invasion. The army wanted to dash ahead, but the navy would not guarantee us broad enough cover. We argued before the Führer, and he decided in favor of the parade. He who later mocked his whole staff and despite their warnings pushed through the Ardennes with flanks exposed, he demurred. Just before he was about to pluck the most luscious fruit of all. Later there were a number of trials, and then Goering's air fiasco, but England, alas, was never crushed. It is rumored among us that, during one of the late suppers in the Chancellery at which the Führer made everybody on his staff talk and quarrel while he held off the Führer decision, he once, only once, expressed regret, and that was over his failure to capitalize on the routing of England at Dunkirk. She was within his grasp. He had her, and then the fear of defeat got the better of him and he desisted. The conquest of France had been too sudden. They thought there was time for a little gloating. Ah, the historical moment! He who fails to grasp it may never have another chance. If only we had sailed against England in strength instead of singing about it. If only."

The generals admitted they were guilty for allowing themselves to be hoodwinked by the Nazis. "It cannot be denied that we of the old Wehrmacht were not unhappy at the coming into power of a nationalist party after all the pacifism of the socialists and communists. We veterans of World War I remember the humiliations we suffered when they tore epaulets off our shoulders and the weaklings at home knifed us in the back. Hitler restored the army to its former prestige. He needed us and we needed him. His brown-shirt people considered us old-fashioned, dressed in a code of honor. We considered his roughnecks not the sort of people to consort with. But he was the state and a soldier is the servant of the state. We serve. We obey. We are apolitical. Of course we had our hard moments. Roehm had the fantasy of an eternal revolution and having his storm-troopers replace our well-exercised drillmasters, who had worked through the lean years of the twenties. Hitler feared that gang, as you know, and so he aligned himself with the General Staff and made a pact. He would not set up a competitive army to rob us of our hard-won dignities. The events of that Roehm putsch are not for polite society. The killing of von Schleicher left some of us ill at ease. But the pact was formed. We got the budget and National Socialism was kept out of the army. No politics, just training and toughening.

"Then the Nazis resorted to their underhand methods. All those who were not blindly for the Führer were against him, they said. What he did with Fritsch was a slap in the face to the whole officer corps. Fritsch was accused by a homosexual of consorting with another, well-known homosexual. Fritsch demanded a court-martial. The Führer would not hear of it. In the end it turned out to be two other homosexuals, but that was the finish of Fritsch. Then there was Blomberg. In his dotage he fell in love with a girl who was on the morals list in Berlin, or at least so they said. Hitler would tolerate no whore on the General Staff. Brauchitsch wanted a divorce. Somebody else needed money. And Hitler held the purse strings and the secret papers. In the end he had something on each and every one of us. Chiefs of staff came and went until he found Keitel and Jodl, men who had never led a company, who spent their time with maps in staff headquarters. Hitler stopped holding war councils and discouraged them in the lower echelons. One chief of staff was giving a pessimistic report and he was fired on the spot before he had finished. But once the war was on, what could we do? *Hannibal ante portas.* Chiefs of staff and generals were numerous, as you realize by the number of those present here, but there was no other Führer.

"When two men met there was always a third among us, and who dared? You know, there were a great many strange rumors in this war. We ourselves never knew how true or false they were. Did you ever hear about the plot to depose Hitler way back in 1938 at the height of the Czech crisis? It may sound melodramatic, but I have it on good authority that members of the General Staff were terrified by our unpreparedness even in the face of the weak Czech army and they were ready to consummate their plot. That very night, before the deed was done, Chamberlain flew to Berchtesgaden and Hitler left Berlin to join him. After the triumph of Munich it would of course have been impossible to justify a putsch to the people.

"And then there is that story about a General Staff plan to embrace the French in an alliance on the basis of equality, get their fleet, and sail against England. It never worked out. The Führer refused. Russia was a fixed idea with him. He thought he could mop them up. A great mistake.

"Toward the end Hitler became ever more capricious. He would issue an order, then when it failed of its purpose would rail against it and ask whose idea it was. It was rather disconcerting to have to remind him that it was his own. That was when we began to keep records of the Führer-decisions. Mostly for our own protection.

"His mania for the offensive knew no bounds. Messerschmitt first brought out his great innovation, the jet plane, in 1943. It was planned as a fighter and it was a fighter, technically the most advanced in the world at the time. One fine day Hitler discovers that it will not be used as a bomber and he casually asks somebody whether it could not be transformed into one. A toady answers, 'Yes, my Führer.' And then for months they toy with bomber racks for the Messerschmitt when everybody knows it is a fighter and not a bomber.

"The same with the v-2. He had to have something to appease the German people, to avenge the terror attacks by destroying London. Instead of putting precious manpower and materials and transport facilities into manufacturing jet planes that would have broken up the Allied bomber offensive, he squandered them on the v-2.

"Against every warning in our history he invaded Russia and started a two-front war that he expected to win before the Americans could move any troops. If only we had stopped and dug in! But he ordered us ever deeper into that boundless landmass. Still, we advanced. Our Iron Crosses arrived on schedule, and a Knight's Cross is not to be sneered at. Then came Stalingrad, and the German soldier lost confidence. Hold on, he was told, the Luftwaffe is on the way. But the longer we stuck it out against the advice of the more experienced generals, the deeper we sank into the sewers of Stalingrad, until finally we were trapped like rats. It was the first of the broken promises. Despair that was once individual crept over us all.

"From then on we squirmed and there were many plans of salvation. Goering wanted to grab Gibraltar, but we never could have lived off of barren Spain, and the roads were as bad as they had been during their civil war. Perhaps we should have taken Malta, but that involved the Italians and you know what they were like."

The dashing, handsome General Otto Hermann Fegelein, who was married to Eva Braun's sister, was the liaison officer between the ss High Command and German Supreme Headquarters. He had managed to spend the last four days of the war with his wife in a Bavarian Alpine chalet. After this brief precaptivity furlough, he gave himself up, announcing that his life meant nothing to him. "Well, your life means nothing to me, either, so we start off on an even footing. And being cold and levelheaded tacticians and strategists, let's play a game tonight, purely in the interests of Clausewitz. Why did you lose the war? To what do you impute your defeat and present unpopularity? There are more wars to be fought and this was a pretty big show. What lessons should be drawn from its history? Tell us of the why and wherefore of disaster. Let's analyze it like the diagnosticians that we are. It's all over now or practically so, and the great American public as well as the Intelligence Service want to know why we won. If you tell us why you lost, I'll tell you why we won. Nothing you say will be held against you. It's between you and me. How could it be that a great nation led by an exemplary Führer got knocked out after the first twelve years of a thousand-year reign? Let's lay the maps on the table."

"I was only a liaison officer between Himmler and Hitler and I don't know very much about what really went on. My primary function was to represent the ss at Hitler's headquarters. The ss is one of the most maligned bodies of men in the world. They say that we had special privileges. It's a lie that the old Wehrmacht generals are spreading about us. ss men had extra duties and tougher discipline, not privileges. The ss divisions were thrown into the most dangerous sectors to fill the breach. We suffered the most casualties. Maybe the uniforms issued to us were somewhat better, and the food. But the ss man was made of sterner stuff. We did not conduct war as in the days of the Old Fritz, from rear echelons, with commanders living in luxury. In an ss division no command posts ten kilometers behind the lines. Our system provided for command posts right up front with the men. We embodied real comradeship, not the generalship of the Old Fritz exemplified by men who sat in headquarters poring over maps and drawing paper plans.

"The ss formally lodges a complaint against the German Air Force. If there had only been ss units in the Air Force it would never have come to the sorry state it did under that blusterer Goering. He ought to be condemned to death for what he did. Our planes were grounded by your air superiority and he filled the airfields with boys who slept in barracks and did nothing but clean and scrub and have a good time. They never knew what it meant to suffer a winter in the east sleeping unsheltered in the cold. They always had their warm bunks. Goering was forever promising us more planes, new planes. In the meantime he hogged the men, just kept them around on airfields doing nothing or fiddling with ack-ack guns when they should have been learning to shoot. We needed this flower of German manhood and he kept them stored up, always promising that his planes would get off the ground. If you want me to give you one single reason for our defeat I would say it was Hermann Goering and I hope you hang him."

"Now that we know why the air force brought you defeat and us victory, tell me about your boss. What was the secret of Himmler's success?"

"Beyond a doubt one thing: regular habits. He always got up in the morning at the same hour and worked through the day."

The captive generals, who had all been registered in due form, freely responded to any casual or formal questioning, though in the last days we were not very interested in a stray headquarters staff that belonged to a corps existing only on paper. There were still a few hundred thousand men in the field in the southern sector, but they were mostly ragtag elements.

American officers drinking in a separate apartment had been discussing the terms of surrender of Army Group G under Field Marshal Kesselring when a jeep drew up with two innocuous-looking Luftwaffe youths. "Why are you bringing them here? This place is reserved for generals. That's a sergeant and a PFC. Take them to the cage or tell them to go home. Who wants them?" But the two were of interest despite their lowly rank. "OK, I'll take the PFC first. When were you captured?"

"We were shot down about two hours ago."

"By whom?"

"By your ack-ack."

"And what were you doing over our lines four hours after the surrender of Army Group G?"

"I don't know. The sergeant was the pilot. I was only told to get in and shut up."

"Destination?"

"I don't know."

"The two-kilogram dynamite charges found in your school training plane, what were they for?"

"I don't know. Honestly I don't."

"Where did you come from? What airfield?"

"Somewhere around Salzburg."

"Where around Salzburg? North, east, south, west?"

"I don't know. I was only brought there this morning."

"When did you leave?"

"About two hours ago."

"Were there other planes with you?"

"One or two."

"What type?"

"Arados, training planes."

"And what was your mission?"

"I swear I don't know. On my word of honor I don't know."

Neither photomaps, nor cajoling, nor the little deceits in which interrogators indulge yielded anything. After a while you either believe the POW or you don't and usually you do. POWs do not lie. At least not unless they are fools and then they are not interesting.

The sergeant, who was called next, was blond and lean, with delicate features. None of that hard bulging muscle and jutting jaw. The beardless face was almost effeminate. He had not marched across Europe, he had flown. His uniform, though old, was clean and well-kept.

"Name?"

"Hans Tolsch."

"Rank?"

"Unteroffizier."

"Where were you born?"

"You can see my paybook."

"Deggendorf. That's not far from here."

Silence. Waiting.

"Well, I see they sent you out to do a little postarmistice job."

"What do you mean?"

"You know that an armistice covering the whole front was signed with Army Group G at 1200, and you took off at 1400, two hours later, to do a little behind-the-lines playing with us. Where did you take off from?"

Silence.

"Two-kilogram charges of TNT can be a nuisance."

Silence.

"See here, my boy. It's all over. It's finished. They surrendered at 1200. What you did has no status in international law. You're a behind-the-lines operative to us. Your own army cannot protect you. It's a violation of the surrender terms just signed."

"I did as I was ordered."

"What were you ordered?"

Silence.

"You poor slob, why get yourself shot as a spy on the day the war is over, when you've got a lifetime ahead of you?"

"The war is not over."

"I'm telling you it is. It's over; they signed this morning and you were sent out two hours later. Don't you ever want to go home?"

"Yes."

"But you won't if you're stupid in this way. You're not a POW; in peacetime you're a saboteur with no protection from your own government or the Geneva Convention."

"You're too interested. If the war were over you would not be asking me questions."

Touché, my boy. "Listen here. Are your parents alive?"

"Yes."

"And when did you last see them?"

"Three months ago. You can see in my paybook under furloughs."

"Don't you want to see them again?"

Silence.

"Deggendorf is a rather pretty town."

The young man was tense. And I, the interrogator, was sweating. That son of a bitch. After the PFCs and lieutenants and generals who talked and talked and talked, beat their gums until you had to shut them up, wept, whined, and tried to use the interrogation chamber as a confessional box, laying bare their souls to the first sympathetic auditor to whom they could speak without fear of reprisal, after all these guys who abused the privilege and yapped on and on under a compulsion to participate in the mass treachery, to tell what they should not tell, to unburden themselves, relieve themselves on your table — after all the useless chatter, this son of a bitch shuts up like a clam.

He's making a fool of me. I'll lose face. What is he trying to do? I'll kill the bastard. I don't want one of our guys to wake up with his tank blown from under him or an arms depot going up in the air killing hundreds of our boys. Damn the Geneva Convention! Those bastards play peace, peace, and then come throwing little dynamite charges around, and expect us to send them home in a convoy. Like the bastards that would first shoot at us every damn round they had, knocking off our boys, and then, when there were no more left, come out with uplifted arms to be taken to chow in the POW cage.

This one won't get away with it. Think of our boys. Damn the paper. I'll kill the bastard. And then lose face. What will the colonel say? You just can't do those things at Corps. "Boy, time is getting short. I want to know what field you left from, where you were to land, who sent you on this scatterbrained mission, what you were to do, how many other planes left the same field. If you make it difficult it will be tough on you. You know you all talk in the end."

"Go ahead, beat me, kill me. You can beat me to death. You will see. You won't get anything out of me. I am a man of character. I do not want to consider myself a swine after the war."

"There won't be any after the war for you if you persist in being an idiot."

Nothing works, none of the stories about Murmansk and the salt mines of Siberia. Nothing in the measly stock-in-trade. It will take time, and all the while these little Arados may be landing somewhere, and our boys setting off trip wires and blowing themselves to bits just so that this son of a bitch can preserve his character. He is only trying to work out his own psychological salvation on you. I was losing patience.

At that moment the American staff sergeant announced a newcomer to the captive generals' club — Field Marshal of the Luftwaffe Sperrle, Commander of the Legion Condor that had peppered the cities and towns of Spain during the Civil War, leader of the attack on Guernica, and later director of the blitz against England. Once I had lamented the defeat of Loyalist Spain as the beginning of the end. Now the wheel of fortune had turned and Sperrle was my prisoner, my prime exhibit.

"Come on, you idiot. If I show you Sperrle will you believe that the war is over? You've seen pictures of him. If you now see Field Marshal Sperrle in the flesh will you quit the tomfoolery and save your little neck? I have pity for you, pity." I pulled the kid across the street.

"Yes, that's Sperrle." Man Mountain Sperrle was receiving the homage of his fellow captive lieutenant generals and major generals, while his orderlies fussed with his baggage and looked for a chair that would fit his bulk. Goering sure went for size. "All that proves to me is that Sperrle is now a prisoner along with me. I have my orders."

"Come on in here, you dope. Herr Field Marshal, this simp was sent off in some school plane from the Salzburg air field to place dynamite charges behind our lines. It's all over now. For the poor kid's sake, have him tell us where he and the other lads were to put the stuff."

The old field marshal had deposited himself in an armchair and he spoke to the Unteroffizier from the recesses of his bowels. "Come here, my child." The livid pilot stood at rigid attention. The generals had stopped their small talk. "My child, if I were you, I would take into consideration the request that the American Intelligence Service is putting to you. You are young yet. What you intended to do was honorable. But it is over now. Even if you tied grenades around your waist and threw yourself through a window into an American installation it would alter nothing in the final outcome. We must all bear the burdens of captivity."

The sergeant waited respectfully for the field marshal to finish. Then in a decisive staccato tone: "Sir, I require a direct order from you, to supersede the direct order that I received from my previous commanding officer before I set out on my mission. Unless I receive such a direct order, my lips are sealed by my previous order."

"Your attitude is praiseworthy, my son, but under the circumstances . . ."

"A direct order, sir."

The melodrama of the field marshal and the sergeant was getting us nowhere. Why should our men die for these phony theatrics? "I give you ten minutes. I'm not interested in your German etiquette of orders and counterorders. Settle it between yourselves."

It worked, and I breathed a sigh of relief because I had not the remotest idea what to do next. But it had taken a field marshal to break Sergeant Hans. Duly ordered, he went to work, drew charts and sketches, made up lists of pilots with names and birthplaces, estimated distances and the fuel capacity of various types of training planes. A Captain Schmidt at the airstrip northwest of Salzburg had gotten the bright idea of putting the training school planes to one final warlike use. Each of forty young pilots had been allotted about two hours worth of gas and ordered to land anywhere he wished near his native town. If he landed safely he was to lay the TNT charges near any of our military installations and take off for home and mamma and papa with discharge papers in order. After Hans identified the planes, their probable courses were charted and most of them shot down, either destroyed or captured. Hans was lost in a POW collecting point.

Surfeited on German generals, I went off and got plastered. At six in the morning two protective sergeants put me under a cold shower and then propped me up on an improvised podium, for I was scheduled to deliver a lecture on the organization of the German civil administration, about which I knew nothing. The officers at Corps were ordered to attend and praised my talk for its quiet lucidity. I dared not move my head, fearing lest it drop off. With a group of fellow officers from Corps I spent the rest of the day in the Bavarian Alps. We followed a mountain stream up into hills that were said to be full of ss men, perhaps Werewolves. We titillated ourselves by peering into caves where they might be hiding; stopped stragglers in civilian clothes and asked for their passes; inspected their discharge papers dated 4 May and told them to go home. Nobody wanted anymore ordinary POWs. We stripped and ducked in the icy water, we talked with bravado about what good targets our naked bodies would make if ss men in the cliffs above us wanted to take a last shot. We reminisced about women. Back at our quarters, we ate well and drank champagne, made fun of peace, and got tight on 1830 cognac. At the end of the evening I went to bed and stared at the ceiling.

A few days later I was ordered to pick up Hitler's war diary at Kesselring's headquarters in the Berchtesgadner Hof. The atmosphere there was different from that at Weilheim. The genial field marshal, nominally our prisoner, was running things, and I was no longer a cock of the walk. This was my last encounter with the German High Command and I reflected ruefully on my precipitous fall in status.

The French had been the first to reach Hitler's Eagles' Nest in Berchtesgaden, and they turned the wine cellar into a red sea, breaking every bottle for the hell of it. Nothing was left for us. The furnishings of the place were petty bourgeois, German-style sofas and armchairs in hideous upholstery. I clambered around the junk on the heights and found a bunch of skeleton keys to the guest house and a batch of Martin Bormann's stationery, my war booty. When we came down to the modern, well-appointed Berchtesgadner Hof in the town below we were received at the door by the airborne troops of the USA looking spick and a bevy of German generals looking span, while the hotel managers bustled about, waiters serving Americans and Germans interchangeable platters in adjacent rooms, just as the Geneva Convention stipulated.

Privates were saluting generals and generals saluting privates and maids were running around bedrooms. Everything was immaculate.

At the Berchtesgadner Hof we witnessed the liquidation of the German armies south under the direction of Field Marshal von Kesselring, with German corps generals strutting around and staff people performing their functions with punctilio. "You, Westfall, come at 10 — the American General Devers is due at 9 — and Tolsdorff, you come at 11, and Guderian is to come at 12," ordered the spruce businessman field marshal. The telephone rang. "Pardon me. Oh yes, everything is in order. We mean to observe all the commitments meticulously." He turned to us, apologizing for the interruption. "Sorry, the war diary was burned. See Chief of Staff Wintner about it. They certified to that effect. I sent the War College into the field; I would not have anybody hanging around the rear. Oh, you like our Alps. I do, too." The telephone again. "Pardon me. Yes, Guderian. No, I cannot ask the American authorities to let you take your daily ride. If I made an exception for you, Tolsdorff would insist on a parade each day before breakfast and then where would we be? Confine yourself to pacing indoors."

An affable fellow, this Kesselring. A bumptious man of affairs, gone bankrupt with most of his assets saved, helpful to the new receivers, gracious and witty. Once again the telephone. "Kesselring. Yes! No! Later! Heil Hitler!" He hung up. "And what can I do for you? Oh yes, you wanted the German War College. Where is the War College? Heavens, where did we last put the War College? In some village in the Alps. In Lengries perhaps, or in Saalach. General Spaeth wanted to move elsewhere but I prohibited it. I think he wanted to be with his wife. So would four million other German soldiers.

Rather indecent of him. Well, glad to have met you. Hope you find him. Just look through that mountain area, he's around somewhere."

I did not believe that the war diary had been destroyed. Surely the historians introduced into Hitler's headquarters to record Führer-decisions must have kept a copy somewhere. Eventually we found a charred portion of the original document. With the aid of the stenographers who had taken the notes, we were able to reconstruct a section.

"What was the secret of Hitler's success?" I asked one of the historians who had been in his entourage.

"He was a demon. There was something dynamic and demonic about him. He had the power of simplification, could get to the heart of a problem without being an expert on the subject. He had a colossal memory, knew the exact quantity of every military item expended in the Battle of Verdun. And what he could not remember he expected us to supply at a moment's notice. He would brook no opposition. Rather headstrong, one might say. And most of all he was skilled in playing one of his henchmen against another. Nobody felt secure. He really delighted in their discomfiture. I was once in the room when Himmler and Ribbentrop were having a fight. I looked at Hitler's face and saw him smiling. But he never let them go too far. If two men quarreled one of them would come and get a Führer-decision, which I recorded, and it was binding. In a few days the other one would sneak in and receive another Führer-decision. And then they would have to get together with their Führer-decisions and iron out the difficulties. Complex administratively, but somehow it worked, because they knew that after two Führer-decisions on the same subject they would get into trouble if they did not reach an accord."

A few days after v-e Day, I had written to my wife: "Hitler was the whole show to an extent hardly equaled even by Napoleon. Next Himmler (Fouché) and Goebbels — the other party people and ministers, wind. The general staff not too impressive though more so than the civilian bosses. But Hitler held all the strings."

# 9

## THE FLEETLESS ADMIRAL

**W**HEN ADMIRAL HORTHY was picked up in Castle Hirschberg, where Hitler had held him under house arrest, he created a problem for the troops that captured him. How were they to deal with this admiral without a ship, who had been dictator, officially Regent, of Hungary for a quarter of a century? On Allied lists he figured among the war criminals for his collaboration with Hitler. But he was also the head of a state and normally his fate would be settled by a formal peace treaty. He was still a monarch, to whom Monaco had sent an accredited representative. The American colonel put in charge of the castle behaved toward Horthy as if he were a reigning sovereign, and the colonel was charmed by Horthy's daughter-in-law, who spoke perfect English. Two American generals invited the admiral to tea.

As a mere interrogator attached to the Twenty-first Corps of the Seventh Army, I had no idea who made the decision to assign me a minor role in the playlet about to be enacted — an episode Horthy oddly garbled in his published memoirs. I was sent to the castle to seize the body and deliver it to headquarters in Wiesbaden, leaving the political tangle for wiser men to unravel.

What was Horthy to be told about his transfer? I invented a solution that would absolve the lower echelons of responsibility: Horthy was informed that he was invited to dinner by General Patch and that I would accompany him across the intervening territory from Weilheim to Wiesbaden. To sustain the fiction, someone unearthed a green dress uniform for me that was not decorated with insignia of rank, leaving my status ambiguous: Was I a military or a diplomatic official? Since I had let it be generally understood around the Corps that I was not a marksman of note, a tough little counterintelligence agent was designated to be my driver and to intervene in case of any hitch in the plan.

The admiral insisted that he be attended by his valet, dressed as a proper English gentleman's gentleman of the period between the two wars. Horthy was small in stature, but wiry, with a face that I, an amateur physiognomist, classified as Magyar. After his luggage had been loaded into the trunk of the Mercedes parked in the driveway, the admiral himself walked majestically down the steps of the castle, an apparition from another age. He was clad for the journey in a tweed hunting costume, with knee breeches, a cape, and a Sherlock Holmes cap. Though American officers guarding the castle were present at the departure, nobody frisked either the admiral or his servant, an oversight that left me a little uneasy. Off we rode with the latest map of how to travel to Wiesbaden, but without information on which bridges had been blown up and how we would make the appropriate detours. Since I knew no Hungarian, the admiral quickly suggested that we converse in German. For at least half an hour we bumped along in silence broken only by incomprehensible exchanges between Horthy and his valet, sitting up front with the CIC agent in whom I had invested superhuman powers.

I was at a loss for topics of conversation with Horthy, since instructions on that point had not been issued to me. Ensconced beside this incarnation of a craggy-faced English hunter, I was growing increasingly uncomfortable, when belatedly I recalled that he had once been an aide to the aged Emperor Franz Josef. "Did you know the Esterhazys?" I blurted out. His response was prompt and genial: "Of course. They were favorites at the court of the Emperor." From an evocation of the good old days Horthy launched into a eulogy of the Austro-Hungarian Empire and then, without further prodding, a defense of Hungary's alliance with Germany in World War II. This provoked me to lead a charge against his sacrifice of so many Hungarian army divisions that were dispatched to the eastern front to shield elite German troops facing the Russian advance. Avoiding a direct response, Horthy unfolded the Hungarian policy as a civilized European stand against the barbarian hordes from the east, the stereotypical answer. He had, after all, rejected Hitler's last demand for additional troops. A detailed description of his maneuvers to preserve the independence of Hungary, which had kept the appurtenances of a cabinet, was a prelude to his long justification that ultimately persuaded the Allies to distinguish him from the Nazi war criminals.

It was clear to me at the outset of our encounter that the admiral identified me as a Jew. Half of his monologue was devoted to his protection of Hungarian Jews and his refusal to participate in their round-up by the Nazis. The canny old man had worsted more formidable antagonists than this young American. Tears dramatized his apologia. The sentimental outpouring touched me, and by the time we stopped at Ulm on the Danube, for a moment I felt ashamed for deceiving him. But I swallowed my remorse and continued to press him on the sacrifice of Hungarian divisions when he knew that the war was lost. "What could I do?" pleaded the Regent of Hungary (a POW, or a displaced person, or a war criminal, depending on how you read international law). The old sailor, smelling a sinking ship, had tried to abandon it. The German Foreign Office had left this seventy-eight-year old in the pathway of our advancing armies, at about the time that they arranged for Pétain's delivery.

When Hitler had gotten wind of Horthy's secret emissaries to the Allied command, Hungary was transformed into a protectorate, Horthy's beloved son was abducted, and German troops occupied Budapest. "Hitler kept demanding that I send him more divisions. I stalled with all manner of excuses, requesting the necessary equipment for them before providing the men. He threatened me and then assured me that the arms would be supplied before the battle. In the end I had to deliver the poor men and they were thrown in front of the German troops as a buffer. With their naked breasts they repulsed Russian tanks. They were massacred. I lost twelve or thirteen divisions.

"Then one day I received word to appear before him. I consulted my ministers, for mine was a constitutional regime, on whether I should leave Budapest or not. I did not want to go. I was suspicious, but in the end I had to obey the summons. As soon as I arrived I felt that something was in the air. In his private chambers he told me that my game was up, that he would not risk another Italian fiasco. He said he had complete information about my negotiations with the Allies, and he kept me there while German troops took possession of official installations in Budapest. That was in March 1944. In October they placed me in the castle in protective custody and appointed the former German consul to Monaco as a special representative to give the situation a semblance of legality."

"But if, as you say, you always knew that Hitler wanted to possess all of Europe, why did you play his game as long as you did? Why didn't you break with him before you sacrificed twelve or thirteen divisions on the Russian front?"

The Regent of Hungary shrugged his shoulders like so many German privates to whom I had posed the same fatuous question, and the same long-suffering look imprinted itself upon his face. *"Was konnte ich denn machen?* (What could I do?) I was the helpless Führer of a little state." The admiral's apostrophe brought me back to the banality of Central European power politics. Since he resisted capitulating to Hitler's last demands, in his own eyes he remained a Hungarian patriot and deserved Allied amity and protection.

Our journey took far longer than had been anticipated. The bodily needs of the aged Horthy required frequent stops. When we dismounted at an American army post en route, groups of our soldiers gathered round, curious about the four strangely outfitted creatures. Most of the onlookers thought we were actors in some traveling show put together for the entertainment of the troops, and I did not try to disabuse them of that notion. My green uniform, the old man in knickerbockers, the moviesque valet, the nondescript chauffeur, all supported their presumption.

Back in the Mercedes, Horthy continued his monologue. His doctor was a Jew and he did what he could to save the Jews. My German hadn't lost the Eastern European rhythm of Boston Yiddish, my mother tongue, and the hours I spent with the Lutheran Bible made the resulting speech bizarre; but nothing fazed the old admiral, who had outlived the destruction of an empire, a communist revolution, and a jostling by Hitler.

As the afternoon dragged on, Horthy began to express anxiety that we would be late for dinner, and indeed it was dusk before we drew up in front of General Patch's headquarters. I reported to an officer in charge, and after identifying the personage I had brought, made a feeble effort to vanish into the shadows. When Patch arrived he was informed of the prisoner's name. I was taken aback by the tale that circulated about the general's behavior. Reputed to be a gentle man, he had just returned from Dachau, and in an outburst of rage grabbed Horthy by the collar and pushed him through an open door down the stairs into a cellar. During the following period, as Horthy was passed from one military jurisdiction to another, he experienced different treatment that was determined by the immediate officer in command, since no clear-cut decision had been made as to his status. I was not privy to the secret negotiations that had taken place between Horthy and American agents. In the end he was declassified as a war criminal, an example of the confusion that characterized official policy with respect to heads of states that Hitler had dominated.

It was hard to define an appropriate mode of conduct toward the vanquished foe. In basic training we were taught creeping and crawling, jumping and running, some shooting. American officers learned how to yell a battalion order across a field and memorized instructions about the proper margins of a military letter. The General Staff was well versed in the maneuvers of frontal attacks, single and double envelopment, avenues of approach, and everything else in the books. But nobody told anybody how to treat a conquered general. To shake hands or not to shake. What did Grant do to Lee at Apomattox? Did they not observe many elegancies of the victor and the vanquished and then settle down to a good bull session about the right flank and the left flank? In respecting the dignity of a German general officer in defeat, you preserved the worthiness of the profession of arms. There was no past experience on which to base a Manual for the Behavior of General Officers in Receiving Defeated Regents, Generals, and Field Marshals. Some shook hands and some did not. Some were disdainful and some were secret admirers. In the end Horthy got away with murder, and in a sense I felt myself an accessory. *Was konnte ich denn machen?*

# I O

## FAREWELL TO LEIPZIG

**E**ACH TOP PARTY BOSS of the Reich had his favorite scientist (surrounded by a horde of assistants) laboring in an underground hideout, like a medieval duke his alchemist in the cellar of the castle. And the scientist would tell only his patron — Ley, or Goering, or Speer — of his discoveries. Then the Party boss would bring the product of his protégé's labor to Hitler in order to be vindicated for the extravagant expenditures in which he had indulged. During the end phase of the war all science was amalgamated and placed under the skull and bones of a general of the Waffen ss.

When Berlin itself was threatened, scientists were herded into the forests of Thuringia and their laboratories hastily installed in the bowels of the earth. But this was merely a temporary refuge. As trucks from Detroit bearing Yankee soldiers were about to overrun them, the scientists were spirited away again. Special convoys, guarded by the ss, evacuated them to the south, riding through the blackout of the night to the Alps.

Science had the highest priorities. Shipments of multibarreled rocket guns were abandoned on railroad sidings and precious space on rail transport was preempted for the scientists and their gadgets. Sawmills and textile factories in Sonthofen and Kempten high in the Bavarian Alps were equipped to receive the crated secret weapons.

Rumors multiplied like vermin. There were rocket-propelled, radio-controlled missiles that would break up the Allied bomber formations. There were men who could manipulate jets and homing fuses and airwave frequencies and radar and counterradar and counter-counterradar. There was a freezing shell that had been burst over a flock of sheep in a peaceful meadow and all the animals had dropped dead, blood in the lungs coagulated; Goebbels himself had witnessed the preliminary experiments. The chemists among the scientists were mixing new fluids with an alphabet of names, T-Stoff and A-Stoff and z-Stoff. If they had no high octane for their aircraft, the wild jets and rocket-propelled Messerschmitts would be shot through the air by a brew of newly concocted substances. Each secret was baptized with a pretty code name, a mountain flower like Enzian, or Rhine-daughter, Waterfall, Butterfly. The world would end poetically, fancifully.

In the days before the armistice, scientists were abandoning the crumbling Kingdom. They were changing sides, coming through the lines with new rockets they said could wipe out what had never been wiped out before. After working years for the Reich, they finally realized that they were about to lose the war, so they packed up their infernal machines and took off on a trip to the Americans. Their papers were in order and they could move freely throughout the Kingdom, because they had a letter signed by Himmler himself stating in effect that they were perpetually on secret missions and that nobody should interfere with them.

One day a group of scientists appeared before an American officer and boasted, "In yonder barn we left a mechanism that could destroy us all." And they were passed along through channels until they reached the great pool of science in SHAEF (Supreme Headquarters Allied Expeditionary Force). There the mad and the near-mad were separated from the quasi-sound ones, who were shipped to the United States, it is said, along with a boatload of other Nazi souvenirs.

From Corps headquarters in the building of the Leipzig Fire Insurance Company we sent forth a call: "Do you want to come with us? We are collecting all the scientists in the Kingdom. Orders have been issued from on high to assemble in one place the men of science from the provinces of Saxony and Thuringia, which are to be turned over to the Russians. Be ready by tomorrow at two. Take your wife or mistress if you like and as many personal belongings as you need. Or would you rather be a Russian?"

"No, I would rather be an American."

"Then get to the police station on time."

We loaded them into old GI trucks, veterans of the landings in North Africa and Normandy, and set off toward the west. Go west, scientists, the Russians are coming. What's a scientist? You know, real science — physiology, physics, chemistry. Skip the art and literature and history and philosophy. We've got enough of that ourselves. We're picking German brains. You in the east pick what you can get, we in the west pick what we can get. No looting, boys. We just want the scientist who can transform anything into anything. "Are you an authority on vitamins, or rockets, or chemicals? Well, come along. Are you a technician? Come along." It was a jolly company. There was no coercion, no greater recourse to force than the dangling of a carrot in front of a hare or cheese before a mouse. Of their own free will they piled into the trucks. The genius of science had opted for us. It was like a picnic. We provided the sardines and the bread. And they flocked to us: any scientist who wanted a ride to the west, out of the way of the Russians, climbed aboard. The trucks dashed through the night on the autobahn from Jena to Weimar to Erfurt, twenty packs of German science.

"Never in the entire five-hundred-year history of the University of Leipzig has such an outrage been perpetrated," wrote the rector of the university in a formal protest. "Oh, he is just jealous because he wasn't asked. Rector Schweitzer is an art historian who knows more than any other living man about the Roman portrait under the First Republic."

A few days before our cavalcade departed, a lone scientist who was something of an enigma had turned up at the Leipzig Fire Insurance Company. A wizened little old man, he spoke in hushed tones about his invention that could blow up the whole continent. Though hard-pressed by the Nazis, he had refused to divulge his secret weapon, which was still in process of completion. "What did Hitler mean when he asked God to forgive him for the last eight days of the war? Why did

Hitler say it? The ss themselves were baffled." Gesticulating wildly, the old wizard told us how he had been summoned by the Gestapo and ordered to produce his device before the last eight days of the war because those were to be the Führer's days. But the wizard would tell no one his secret. There were fifteen theoretical principles upon which he had been working and he required three more years for his labors. They banged his head against the wall and put chains upon his feet — he showed us the scars — but he would not divulge anything to the Gestapo. They had been struggling with him since the beginning of the war. In vain had they tried every instrument of power on thought. "Let's distribute the project in the manner of the putting-out system." They begged and cajoled and threatened. He was adamant. "We will give you assistants, doctors, professors, men of industry." But he knew that they wanted only to rob him of his invention. When assistants began to learn too much he swallowed the formulas.

The old scientist preferred to work for private industry, not the state. An international syndicate had approached him clandestinely through a certain Serge Czekali in Switzerland in the name of the International Nickel Corporation and Mc-Cormick and Ford and General Motors, so he said. The syndicate had built laboratories for him in Berne and Prague and Milan and Sofia and Budapest. But the Gestapo was forever on his trail. In desperation he fled to the Crimea, and there in a beautiful villa by the sea he worked in peace on his fifteen principles. All the theoretical problems had been solved and only their practical application was awaiting the toolmaker, when the Gestapo concluded that he was acting against the security of the state and arrested him and threw him into a dungeon. For days after the armistice, the Americans listened to his story, examined his weird drawings and his apparatus, which left everyone who approached it slightly jittery, and no one could say for sure that he was deranged.

The old fellow posed a knotty problem for me. A doctor of philosophy with literary training, I had no way of evaluating his pretensions. My appeal to the chemical officer for enlightenment resulted only in an outraged command that his paraphernalia be transferred immediately from the offices of the insurance company to a vacant lot nearby; if the world was to be destroyed, the epicenter of the explosion was not going to be in his bailiwick. I was left on my own to resolve the dilemma facing me. Should I include my eccentric among the scientists from the University of Leipzig, who had impeccable academic credentials? Should I have him mount one of the waiting trucks? Or should I leave him behind for the Russians? I knew nothing about an atomic bomb or the team that was storming the hill where the German physicist Heisenberg was poised for the arrival of the Americans. The more I listened to my scientist the more I was convinced that I had before me a classic example of a paranoid schizophrenic as described in the textbooks. But what if I were wrong and abandoned to the Russians this repository of the great secret? On the other hand, if I threw him in with the rest of the scientists and his lunacy became apparent, what would my superiors think of me? I would never make the rank of captain. In a final momentous decision, I left the mad one to the Russians rather than risk being thought a fool at headquarters.

Off I went with my twenty truckloads, at the head of a convoy to Wiesbaden along the autobahn that Hitler had built as a one-way road to the west. Since there were far more scientists than we had trucks for transporting them, I had to return for a second batch. The spirits of the potpourri of scientists were high, and many of them assumed they would be directly enrolled in laboratories that the prescient Americans had prepared for them in advance. When later I turned up again in Wiesbaden, I learned that a hierarchy had been promptly established among our passengers. To their minds it was evident that those who had landed in the first contingent were deliberately chosen by the Americans as superior to those remaining for the second, a fortuitous arrangement that was translated into a new criterion of excellence among them.

By the beginning of June 1945, freed from the shackles of strict military censorship, I wrote to my wife from Leipzig: "Here I am at the other end of the accursed country. For some reason that I cannot explain, this particular city has thrown me into a complete state of depression. The sheer quantity of piled-up rubble, in the midst of which people form their orderly queues, ride streetcars and bicycles, gather in groups to exchange black-market goods in very small quantities, welcome released soldiers in an undemonstrative manner, is to me quite maddening. I have driven through scores of wrecked cities, but never walked about in one as large as Leipzig for any length of time. The facades remain standing. And the people do not look either excited or depressed. Up until now I have been quartered in relatively rich agricultural areas. This urban scene is something that I cannot understand. We live in hotels and eat the old c rations. And then we sit in a fire insurance building. I have permission to talk to people in the streets, but either I have lost my cunning or they have nothing to say. Saw a Russian general the other day preparing for the takeover. He looked like a capable businessman, *avec* paunch.

"It is horrible but I have no curiosity — and I have taken refuge in my rooms. In the hotel the atmosphere is similar to a boys' dormitory. The restaurant is more like a university faculty club. The office is not unlike an overstaffed government

agency. If only there were work. But our function is just to occupy space and time.

"It happens that I have neither heard a radio nor seen a
newspaper for a number of days and I have no notion about
what is going on in the world. And if I did read the newspapers I would probably know less. All I can think of is the years
ahead. And there seems to be no way of getting into some
kind of rut that would make living possible. I feel as if I were
in an invisible prison in this place."

In mid-June I was still in Leipzig, chafing at the bit. "I live
among our German enemies and hostile allies. The temper is
as grim as mine on certain Sunday mornings. This military
hangover is something to experience. All I can keep repeating
is that I am bored. I can really understand the eighteenth-
century noble for the first time. You live in a city of at least
five hundred thousand, but enclosed in a court. You see 'the
people' for the first few days, then you begin to hide your eyes
from them. You eat, you smoke. Of course you are deprived
of many of the eighteenth-century noble amusements. The
people have them but not much food. The people are servile,
we are correct. After a while the wreckage escapes the eye.
Well, I talk to scientists and a few industrialists but I always
want to run away. Oh for a few decent POWs!"

Back in 1942 the Wehrmacht and the government bureaus
had devoured tons of paper and the shortage in the Kingdom
was great. Publishers groaned, until they found a secret
cache: not all the forbidden books had been burned; that had
merely been announced for propaganda purposes. In the great
warehouses of the commission dealers in Leipzig were mountains of uncut Heine and Mann and Werfel and Mendelssohn
the composer. Their works were *vermackelt,* ground up, and
once they had been well mashed and the words confused

among themselves the paper was shipped to Max Amann, to be distributed to each according to his loyalty, for a printing of *Mein Kampf* and *Memoirs of a Dead Hero* and drippings of Rosenberg and Goering.

"What would *you* do? Just put yourself in my position. You know that if you do not join the Party they will denounce you to the Gestapo and send you away. Twice I got warnings from them. They said that they would put an agent in my publishing house just as they did in Klemper's. And you know what that means. The end. It was the gravest decision I have ever had to make in my whole life. Was it better for me to close my firm, the last non-Nazi publishing house in Leipzig, the last ray of true culture in Germany, or to join the Party and continue to operate somehow? I made my decision and now I regret it. But what good would it have done if I had died in a concentration camp? You can see by my list of authors that I am not a Nazi. The choicest creations of world literature: Horace, De la Rochefoucauld, Hamann, Swift, St. Augustine, Lucullus. These are not Nazi writers.

"And if you ask me how I got the paper and why they let me continue, it will surprise you. It required diplomacy. I used to say to them, 'Why do you want more editions of Gobineau and Chamberlain and Rosenberg? These already exist in so many deluxe editions with which my firm would never be able to compete. Let me do something different,' I said, 'and besides, it will be good for the foreign trade with Switzerland and Sweden.' You will never know the difficulties I had getting paper. But I hid a bit here, falsified a return there, and somehow I continued. Now I am labeled a Nazi. But does not the Bible say, 'By their works thou shalt know them'? I am not one of those who say this today and another thing tomorrow. What can I do to wipe away the stigma?"

Toward the end people wearied of Nazi Party literature. It would not sell. And this cheese was disdained by the men at the front. They wanted good old stories by Gottfried Keller and Conrad Ferdinand Meyer, nineteenth-century tales of the fat bourgeois. What, no Nietzsche in your knapsack? No Nietzsche. A few Goethes here and there and even a bit of Hegel; but no *Mein Kampf.* The Party literature approved by the Book Publishing Sections of the Cultural Chamber gathered dust, while German soldiers clamored for translations of *Gone with the Wind* to comfort them through long nights in cellars and foxholes and pillboxes.

"What do you want to read? 'Hansel and Gretel'?"

"Books about American Indians are what we enjoy. Novels about love are what we want."

When peace came the people had nothing to read in their vast prison. The bragging about victory had left a bitter taste.

Despite the ample supplies of liquor with which American officers were rewarded for their heroic and unheroic achievements, the boredom of war lay heavily upon us as the stay of the United States Army in Leipzig was prolonged. Since there was nothing better to do, I teamed up with a British colonel to see how we might collect the books published during the war in Leipzig, an official depository, and send them to the Library of Congress and the British Museum. Having ensconced ourselves in the local police headquarters, we ordered the publishers to appear at stated intervals, bringing with them lists of their wartime production. We played games, setting the appointments at arbitrary times such as 6:09. To our amazement, our summonses were obeyed with punctuality and without complaint, until one gentleman entered the office, neatly placed his gloves on the table, and with an Oxford accent inquired in a supercilious tone whether we were paying for the books or confiscating them. Even the imminent arrival of the Russians under the arrangement that mandated turning over to them Saxony and Thuringia did not seem to faze this dandified publisher. But an abrupt change in our previously amiable manner intimidated him into verbal compliance. We thought we had assured the delivery of a copy of each book to our respective national libraries. We were determined to salvage the refuse of German culture in spite of itself. The lists were carefully prepared, but we never learned whether in fact the books were dispatched.

The Sunday before the transfer of command to the Russians, the *Johannespassion* was performed in Bach's Thomaskirche. Eisenhower's rule was observed in public places: the Germans sat on one side of the aisle, the Americans on the other, no fraternization. Outside the church Russian emissaries were hanging signs across the road welcoming the victorious Soviet troops. The only area that was open to all nations was the zoo, a pitiful spectacle. The most ferocious beasts of the jungle lay languid, starving while the victors and the vanquished strolled to and fro in deathly silence.

Lieutenant Frank E. Manuel recieves the Bronze Star from
Major General Frank W. Milburn, Seventh Army, XXI Corps,
Gmünd, Germany, April 20, 1945

NOTE ON THE AUTHOR

FRANK E. MANUEL reported from Spain for *The Nation* on the
eve of the Spanish Civil War, and has taught at Harvard, Bran-
deis, and New York Universities. He was Eastman Professor at
Oxford, and visiting professor at Hebrew and Chicago Universities, and at the University of California at Los Angeles and at San
Diego. He has been a member of the American Academy of Arts
and Sciences since 1965. Though this is his first book for a general audience, he is the author of fifteen academic works, and
the editor of a handful more. In 1993, he and his wife Fritzie P.
Manuel won a National Book Award for their seminal text
*Utopian Thought in the Western World.*

A NOTE ON THE BOOK

THE TEXT for this book was composed by Steerforth Press
using a digital version of Perpetua, a typeface designed by Eric
Gill and first issued by the Monotype Corporation between
1925 and 1932. All Steerforth books are printed on acid free
papers and this book was bound with traditional smythe sewing
by BookPress~Quebecor of Brattleboro, Vermont.